Living by Faith,

Dwelling in Doubt

Living by Faith,
Dwelling in Doubt

A Story of Belief, Uncertainty,
and Boundless Love

KYLE R. CUPP

LOYOLA PRESS.
A JESUIT MINISTRY
Chicago

LOYOLA PRESS.
A JESUIT MINISTRY

3441 N. Ashland Avenue
Chicago, Illinois 60657
(800) 621-1008
www.loyolapress.com

Cover art credit: Carrie Gowran and Kathryn Seckman Kirsch

Back cover author photo credit: Desiree Chapman

ISBN-13: 978-0-8294-3894-9
ISBN-10: 0-8294-3894-7
Library of Congress Control Number: 2013943381

Printed in the United States of America.

13 14 15 16 17 18 Bang 10 9 8 7 6 5 4 3 2 1

For Genece

Contents

Prologue

A Faith Lost and Found

We needed to talk. In the late evening, with our son in bed and the nighttime chores complete, my wife and I, although exhausted, sat on the couch to talk about the state of our union, our plans for the future, and where we were situated at that time. The subject of our faith came up, and I admitted to her in a solemn, confessional tone that I couldn't say for sure whether or not I still believed in God. Until I stated the words, I didn't know the extent of my doubts, but with the words spoken and heard, my unbelief became real. Looking into my wife's glistening eyes, I could tell that my confession didn't please her. It didn't please me. I felt distant from God and even from the idea of God, more so for having made a confession of unfaith to another person, someone I deeply loved and did not wish to hurt.

Before meeting and marrying me, Genece (pronounced Jen-ees) had entered a monastery and become a Franciscan sister. For almost five years, she devoted her life to the monastic way, but before she took her final vows, she gained the relative certainty that her vocation lay elsewhere. She left the monastery and enrolled at Franciscan University, in Steubenville, Ohio, as a nontraditional student.

I was there in graduate school at the time. While on my way to the library one sunny day, I chanced to run into a friend and mention that I needed a part-time job for the summer. My friend suggested the university bookstore, which was then accepting applications. I applied the first chance I got, started working when not in class or playing video games, and befriended a young woman who also worked there. Our bosses thought Genece and I would make a cute couple, so they orchestrated a staff bowling night at which everyone would leave after the first game—everyone except us. We were mindful of their setup, but we didn't mind.

The circumstances of our coming together could very easily have been otherwise. Had I left one building on campus a minute sooner or later, I might never have thought to apply at the bookstore, and I might not have met my wife. Had our friends not plotted to set us up, our relationship might not have taken flight. Our meeting and falling in love seemed to both of us to have a divine hand behind it.

So during our conversation at home that evening, for me to drop upon her shoulders my doubts about my belief in God was no small affair—our marriage had begun and had remained a state of life in the church. I assured her that I had no plans to stop attending Mass or any desire to stop raising our son, Jonathan, in the faith. My uncertainty was no cause for such decisive action. I felt distant from God and even the idea of God, perhaps more so than I ever had before; old images of God that had once consoled me remained silent, their faces unseen but for memory. I felt as though I no longer had a Father in heaven who had sent his Son to show me his love. If I prayed at all, it was to Vivian, the daughter we had lost, for her intercessions, but she felt far away as well. I felt worlds apart from most people.

Over the following few months, God still felt absent, but no more or less than when my doubts began. I went to Mass as a wager, my participation predicated on the possibility of God rather than on a manifestation of God's presence. I enjoyed the liturgy and seeing friends afterward, but I was ceasing even to care whether or not I had a relationship with God. With continuing news reports of scandal and corruption, I grew cynical and started joking that my church was the religious wing of the multidimensional evil law firm Wolfram & Hart from the television show *Angel*.

During this time of walking in darkness, two things happened that reilluminated my way. The first was the birth of our daughter Mirielle. The joy and gift of new life helped soften my heart, and she, like her brother, was so full of love and wonder and energy that I could not help but see the God I loved in her giggles and eyes and puckered lips. Intellectually, though, I remained apprehensive about the idea of God.

It was also during this time that I happened to revisit some post-modernist writers, specifically some religiously minded ones. I thought about my dwindling faith in terms of the fragmentation of my life and the "otherness" of God. I was reminded that faith has always played a role in my life and did so long before I embraced a religious faith. God appeared on the horizon. I started praying more again, and if doing so still felt odd, it at least felt right.

In Mark Helprin's novel *A Soldier of the Great War*, the protagonist, Alessandro Giuliani, says that God is not proved in argument but is apprehended in the beauty of a sad song, in the love of a child, and in the mortification of the flesh. Sometimes he sees; sometimes he doesn't. It's the same for me.

God may not make rational sense to us in an age that no longer speaks with an overarching religious vocabulary, and I'm not sure he makes sense to me. Sense or no, it doesn't matter. I'm not going to try to make sense of God. I'm just going to strive each day to pray, and fast, and love.

1

A Loss, Faced with Hope

I never looked into the face of our first conceived child. Francis Estel never grew a face. The little jellybean never grew arms or legs or a head. If the heart ever formed and beat, we never heard it.

Genece's first known pregnancy ended during the first trimester. We were crushed, and we wept. It was the first time I had cried in many years. Tears did not come easily to me, although parenthood has since changed that some. After returning home with the news heavy in our hearts, my wife and I both fell to the floor, and our tears flowed until our eyes were red and wounded with grief.

For a year we had tried unsuccessfully to conceive. Stress and low progesterone kept new life at bay. We were aware that Genece's pregnancies, if they came, would always be classified as high risk, but this inevitability did not kill our hopes. We allowed ourselves to feel overjoyed when a pregnancy test showed us our first positive, but I remained hesitant to give my heart away fully, my faith still a little weak. We both knew that getting through the first trimester would be a trial, and Genece took care to rest and give the new life all the help she could.

Six weeks into the pregnancy, we went in for a scheduled doctor's visit and a sonogram. It is possible, though not always the case, that a heartbeat can be seen at six weeks, so we knew this visit would tell us nothing certain if no heartbeat could be detected. We nonetheless really wanted to hear it and know that our child was alive and well. To our dismay, no beat could be heard or seen.

Genece had irregular bleeding, so her doctor put her on bed rest. I brought her communion on Sundays since she couldn't make the trip to Mass, short though it was. We were living in San Antonio, Texas, at the time, in a small, cramped apartment. Genece lay in bed, sometimes reading, sometimes watching *The Lord of the Rings* movies straight through, always miserable but holding on to a sliver of hope.

A couple of weeks later, when a heartbeat, if present, was sure to be seen, we went for another sonogram. Nothing. Genece's doctor sat us down and solemnly told us that she would not be delivering our baby. I sat, stoic, and thanked her for her help and all she had done for us, but I looked only at my wife. At the news, then spoken, then confirmed, her body shook, her cheeks shuddered, and her mouth trembled into the most terrible frown I had ever seen. Her eyes swelled and reddened, and she sobbed.

My heart would have hardened into something dead to the world had I not kept my eyes on my wife's face and taken her hands in mine. Her face revealed her grief and her sorrow and showed me someone new, someone I had not fully met before. I could not look away because I saw behind her flooded eyes and crestfallen frown a heart broken yet still beating with hope, hope for a heart that would not beat with life on this side of eternity—hope for the future and for us. I fell in love all over again with my beloved wife and with our beloved deceased. I kept the faith that love made sense amid such loss. In her grief, Genece gave me the grace to keep going.

Unsure of whether we had conceived a boy or a girl, we named the child Francis Estel—Francis after the famous saint of Assisi we both venerated. Estel we took from Tolkien's famous novel. In the appendix to *The Lord of the Rings*, Tolkien told at greater length the sad but triumphant love story of Aragorn and Arwen. As a child, Aragorn had been given a new name to hide his identity from enemies that pursued him: Estel. It meant hope.

2

Shattered Stories

Imagine yourself in a great cathedral that's adorned with many majestic stained-glass windows, each depicting the life of a saint. One of these speaks to you more than the others. You stare at the entire image between the frames and admire how it has captured important moments in the saint's life and, by placing them together, revealed the wholeness of a person.

Next you turn your attention to the various scenes. You marvel at each of these in turn, taking your time to let the light and color leave a lasting impression on your imagination. You gaze reverently for so long that the image has now changed slightly with the shifting of the sun's rays. The light alternates between immense brightness and pale dimness with the movement of the clouds.

As you are returning your attention to the whole image, hoping that your study of each part will allow you now to see something new, the ground begins to shake beneath you, and the walls vibrate violently. Before you have a chance to seek cover, the stained-glass window shatters, the pieces fall before you, and the sun glares into the church like an unwelcomed visitor.

The quake stops and you look down at the shattered story at your feet. The shards, though still beautiful, are sharp to the touch. You recognize the fragments of different stories scattered upon the floor, but they no longer make the sense they once did. No level of repair will bring them together. The pieces exist but as fragments of a story now lost to memory.

This image is one of the ways in which I think about my life. I live in the sharp fragments of shattered stories. I walk among them, picking them up, trying to make sense of them even while being cut by their edges.

I was born to a Buddhist father and a somewhat-lapsed Catholic mother. This meant that I had a bewildering and contradictory theological upbringing. Each of my parents told me radically different stories about the almighty and the everlasting, setting before me divergent paths for my walk of faith.

I must have been interested in what they both had to say, because I recall asking each of them for a second opinion on all matters of the otherworldly. Whether minutes or months had passed I cannot remember, but sometime after hearing from my mom that God became man in the person of Jesus Christ, I went into the master bedroom, where my dad was getting out of bed, and posed the question, pointedly and without any preface or segue: "Is Jesus God?"

As Dad sat in bed, waking up, blinking, and gathering his thoughts, my eyes fell to the little statue of Buddha he had placed on the nightstand. I had asked him about that statue before.

"I believe Jesus existed," he answered, "but not that he was God. He was a very important prophet, but nothing more."

I didn't really know what that meant, but I grasped enough to ascertain that my parents did not agree about Jesus or about God. They also disagreed about the devil. Demons would later feature prominently in my mom's telling, at least to this boy's active imagination, but in my dad's they never set their hoofed feet upon the stage. I seem to recall my father denying the devil existed.

With these incompatible stories in hand, I regularly sought out a quiet place to think . . . and then think . . . and then think some more. I did a lot of thinking as a young child. The oft-pondering Winnie the Pooh was a hero of mine.

Adding to my confusion, my parents divorced when I was four, and with their separation came two conflicting accounts of what had happened and why. They each would give me censored and abridged reports about their loss of love, their growing apart, and their physical separation. My mother's and father's explanations did not add up to a coherent chronology. My life subsequently became a puzzle whose pieces didn't fit properly together. Split apart, I would now have two homes, two families, and two identities. My place in the world felt unstable, like ground jostled by the earthquakes that would sometimes shake the foundation of my Southern California home.

No longer the son of Joseph and Gretchen, I was now the son of Joseph and the son of Gretchen. My younger brother, Ryan, and I spent some days with one parent and some days with the other. Each residence became more than a separate setting of family affairs; each became a world unto itself, with its own events, activities, emotions, and values, where the other parent was distant and usually not mentioned without lingering awkwardness. In a sense, I was a different person at each place because each world framed and formed my identity in a different way.

For example, the rules of each household differed notably, and my behavior followed suit. My father allowed us to watch movies that my mother would have rightly deemed inappropriate. Some were impressively horrific. The devil may not have existed in my father's telling, but as I got a little older, frightening ghosts and monsters appeared occasionally on his television. I would sometimes stay up late, alone with ghouls and poltergeists and lots of screams, afraid that if I turned off the movie and fell asleep before midnight, I might die at the stroke of twelve. I've no recollection of where I got this idea, but it kept me anxiously curled up on the sofa, transfixed in turn upon the television and the clock. Go figure, though: no movie scene scared me so much as the cartoonish, wacky, face-changing episode in *Pee-wee's Big Adventure*.

When I search for memories of playing with my favorite toys, more images from my time at my father's home come to mind, perhaps because my time with him was more often than not time spent doing my own thing. Departing from my father's home meant saying goodbye to my old man and the *Star Wars* action figures and other toys that belonged at his house. Toys populated my mother's home as well, but I have fewer memories of those and more of our family interactions at dinner, family outings, and, later on, prayer and church. My mother took a more active approach to parenting.

One early morning in 1987 I was stepping into my mom's car for the ride to school when the ground began to shake. Apples from the trees that lined our driveway fell from the branches, hitting the car and the pavement. I was used to earthquakes, but with the driveway shaking and the whole car jostling and the apples falling from above me, this quake put me into a panic. Its epicenter was a mere ten or so miles from where we were.

My mom ushered Ryan and me back inside the house and promptly had us sitting in prayer for the safety of our stepdad, who at that moment would have been driving through a tunnel or on one of the rippling freeways. This would not have been the reaction of my dad, and had I been with him, I don't know that I would have taken the moment to pray. I acted differently around each parent, but in neither case did I consciously pretend to be someone other than myself.

As the years passed, I grew up hearing incompatible stories about the here and the hereafter, about the visible and the invisible. Being the audience of multiple, conflicting narratives, I faced a crisis of belief, at least to the extent possible for a young boy. What was the truth? Who spoke it? Even in early childhood, I wandered about in a dark cloud of unknowing.

As the divorce proceedings would have it, I spent more of my time with my mom, and so it's not surprising that she proved to have more influence on my religious upbringing. Besides, my dad wasn't the proselytizing sort. He still had the statue of Buddha placed on the nightstand by his bed, and he would gladly answer my inquiries and curiosities, but he never, so far as I can remember, actively sought to raise me as a Buddhist. My rearing in the Catholic faith wouldn't begin in earnest for some years after the divorce. I was about eight before my mom got right with the church and had me baptized and receiving Holy Communion.

With my mother's return to her faith, my past became a different world from my present. From kindergarten to second grade, I had gone to a private Christian school and made friends with kids who came from all sorts of religious backgrounds. We ran around the playground being silly and mischievous, tormenting girls on the swing sets and smelling one another's flatulence to determine whose was the most foul—typical boy stuff. Suddenly, in third grade, I found myself attending a private Catholic school and making friends with other Catholics.

Regular Mass and sacraments gave form to this new world. My friendships here had settings beyond the playground: the church on weekends and special parish events at other times. It was here in this new Catholic world that I made my first best friend, Christopher. His family had come from the Philippines and its strong Catholic heritage. Christopher lived within walking distance from my house, and he had a Nintendo Entertainment System before I did, so I took off for his residence as frequently as I could. You could say that video games were my other religion, and Christopher was my fellow communicant.

I cannot tell you who I am as if the answer were one coherent story. My memory would fail me, and even if I could recount every fact and every detail, too much remains unknown to me and too much makes sense only within the context of one setting or another. Despite my leanings and inklings, I have never decided between my parents, choosing to trust one fully and the other one not at all. Objectively, they could not have both been right, but from their respective places and perspectives, each may have spoken truly.

All history, including personal history, incorporates fact, interpretation, and imagination. My parents couldn't have given me the bare reality of their dissolution of marriage even if they had desired to do so. They perceived and remembered the facts differently, they interpreted the significance of them differently, likely both consciously and unconsciously, and they each distinctly imagined the events that drew them apart. Besides, I was a child. Audience matters for what is said and left unsaid. Illuminating me on every fight, frustration, and felt emotion would have been inappropriate, to say the least.

When I look back, the apparent divergence of their stories is not a problem that I must set out to solve. I have no need now to make them converge, and I have no power to do so. They are the fragments of a story I have lived, made my own, and made into something new, but only after interpreting and imagining them from my own place. They are stories that have contributed to who I am and who I am becoming. My wayward way was set by these early events and experiences. When I speak about my faith, I speak from this broken path.

For reasons I hope to make clear, I cannot make complete sense of these shattering events, not a sense that satisfies me. Like a tremor in my soul, they came and passed, leaving no certain explanations. My faith is not about finding explanations for them or making perfect sense of them. Rather, what I call my faith is my choice to live in the drama of these shattered stories, these fragments of a whole life that cannot be put back together.

My faith began not as a religious response to God, either real or imagined, but as my way of navigating the uncertainty between the conflicting words and worlds of my parents. My faith began as a way of being—a manner of walking between two roads when I couldn't simply choose one or the other. My faith originated as a response to the fragmentation of my life.

St. Paul wrote to the Corinthians that we cannot see the whole of reality, for we see and know and understand only part of the truth. Not being God, we see in a mirror dimly, a glass darkly. I would add that we see through shattered stained-glass windows. *To see with faith is not to see the whole but to believe that something of the whole is shown in the fragments we can see.* To live by faith is to live for the whole having only the fragments, some of which have fallen where we cannot reach. We need faith because, without seeing the whole, we cannot fully understand the place and arrangement and meaning of the parts we can see. We try to make sense of events and experiences in our lives without the benefit of the big picture.

In our efforts to live for the whole, we tell stories. The human condition has always involved our telling stories, sharing them, and living according to them. We explain who we are individually by telling our stories, and we do this as well in communion with others. As Richard Kearney says in his book *On Stories*, we tell stories when others ask us who we are.[1]

Storytelling binds us with others: we understand our own lives with and through the stories of others. I cannot tell my story without also telling the stories of my wife and children, and the stories of my parents, and the stories of the communities of which I've been a part. Stories make a person and a people.

Both the telling of stories and the hearing of stories are choices of faith. In telling your story, you decide what to say and how to say it, and you must do so without sure guidance or a final formula. You have to trust and hope that your story expresses the reality you endeavor to convey. In hearing your story, I have to decide how best to interpret it and whether to believe it.

The plurality of stories challenges our faith. Believing one story can be trial enough, but what happens when we're asked to believe multiple, differing stories about the same event or person? There is, for example, no single master Gospel narrative, but four stories, each one different from the others because the author of each fashioned, organized, highlighted, and juxtaposed events and images from the standpoint of his own situation. You can't take the four stories and put them into a coherent whole.

The church, you'll notice, does not try to combine these Gospels. In the Christian tradition, each Gospel reveals its own situated truth. Each is differently true. The Gospel truth is plural, even while gesturing toward a unified whole, specifically toward a single divine person. The Christian believes each of the accounts, not despite their differences, but in accordance with them.

It is a modern prejudice that seeks to make all ways of expressing truth into one master system. A handful of modern critics will point to inconsistencies among Gospel accounts and believe they've undermined their narrative credibility. But the four Gospels are not one way of narrating the life of Jesus Christ.

In the tragically short-lived television show *Firefly*, Shepherd Book walks in on River Tam, whose mind is unmatched in the universe, editing and tearing pages out of Shepherd's Bible. Incredulous, he asks her what she's doing.

"Fixing your Bible," she answers, exasperated at the task before her. The inconsistencies and logic of the Scriptures baffle her, so she has set out to repair the "broken" Bible. Some sections she has removed; others she's marked with suggested changes to make it all work.

"Noah's ark is a problem," River declares before offering some theory of quantum mechanics as a way of fitting thousands of animals onto one boat.

Shepherd Book says that the Bible isn't about making perfect sense but about faith. "You don't fix faith," he tells her. "It fixes you."

I would say that faith doesn't fix you so much as it gives you the fortitude to press on in your brokenness. But Shepherd Book's underlying lesson is spot on. To live according to a plurality of stories means living with tension and inconsistencies and irreconcilable differences, sometimes because the fragments tell a false tale or conceal much more than they reveal, often because each fragment, taken in hand, becomes a new way of looking at the whole, disclosing something different about a reality that passes all understanding.

Shattered stories are part of the human condition. People have dealt with fragmentation and uncertainty since the beginning of our species. The mixed religion and divorce of my parents turned out, in time, to be gifts, for they prepared me for living by faith in our fragmented, uncertain world.

3

Love Has No Time Constraints

I have witnessed death only once: the death of my daughter Vivian.

My wife's pregnancies are classified as high risk. We knew this even before losing our first child just ten weeks into the pregnancy. Perhaps as a way of lessening the impact of anticipated blows, I tend not to get my hopes up about a new arrival in the family until we're well into the second trimester, and even then I hesitate to allow the full excitement that naturally comes with being an expectant parent. For me, the start of pregnancy is a time of hope and dread, a time of brutal uncertainty about life and death. My heart aches and beats restlessly, and I struggle to have faith so that I can love truly in the face of my child's possible demise.

On the Wednesday of Holy Week in 2009, my heart broke. We were expecting our third and were slightly nervous about an irregularity in the shape of the head detected in the sonogram two months earlier. The technician administering today's ultrasound went through the process as normal and was supremely nice, but she refused to respond directly to our promptings about any continuing irregularities. She could tell us the child's sex, however, which we opted to hear: a girl. We were thrilled, but a few minutes later, my wife's doctor, a young man about my age, broke other news.

Our daughter had a rare neural-tube defect known as anencephaly. Parts of her skull and brain had not formed and would not do so. She was still alive, kicking and squirming, especially after my wife ate sugary foods, but her life would be very short. If she lived until term and through the delivery, which was doubtful, she would be with us for only a few hours, perhaps a day or two. My wife was due in September, so we faced the prospect of a long road ahead as we prepared simultaneously for our daughter's birth, baptism, and burial.

I admit that a part of me wanted this unwelcomed journey to be over sooner rather than later, but I also desired and hoped to hold my daughter, to listen to her newborn cries, to hold my wife as she nursed our hungry child, and to share as a family those few precious moments of her life before we would have to say good-bye. We kept the name we had planned on giving her: Vivian, which means "full of life." When we announced the sad news, we were met with condolences and kindnesses from family, friends, parishioners, acquaintances, and even strangers. To our gratitude, Genece's doctor treated Vivian like any other expectant child, gave us free sonograms so we could share what time we could, and consoled us with what guidance he could give.

The words of one friend stood out and have given me resolve since the moment I first read them. He said that love is not constrained by time.

In a way, this statement sums up my faith. I believe in a love that is not constrained by time but that has eternal significance and power, even in the here and now. Faith allows us to love those who are entering or have passed into the uncertainty of death. Enthused by faith, our love follows those we love *into* death, affirms them in their passage, and remains devoted to them after they are gone. I believe that God is this love and that God made this love manifest in the person of Christ. The gospel is a story of love eternal, of love unconstrained by time, love that journeys into the darkness of death. The Gospel narratives point to an unseen future, an everlasting time beyond death and the end of the world, but I submit that its significance pertains especially to the present, to the occasions before us each day that call for a response of love.

In a way, it is we who have to make the Gospels meaningful, because their meaning is not meant to be contained in the covers of a book, however well read. The Scriptures function fully as revelation when we reveal the love of Christ in what we say and do. The Bible, without readers who love, is just a book on the shelf. Faith without works is dead.

The Scriptures testify to a love called for whether we're simply passing strangers on the sidewalk, living next to neighbors, attending to the needs of a friend, or involved in an ugly dispute with someone we passionately dislike. The span of time, whether seven seconds or seventy times or seven years, makes no difference. Love is eternal; it is unconstrained by time.

I grant that this ideal of love sounds lovely, maybe too lovely, like something out of a fairy tale. Is it really worth loving, worth making yourself vulnerable, when the time you have to share and suffer that love may be little more than nothing at all? Common sense suggests that the situation my wife and I found ourselves in—an unborn daughter who would die shortly after birth, if she lived even till then—would not call for the outpouring of self that Jesus associated with love. Genece's doctor told us that one of the reasons we don't have reliable statistics on the likelihood of unborn children with anencephaly living until term is that most people opt for abortion at the diagnosis.

Why go through possibly months of heartbreak and brokenness on the slight chance of being able to hold a baby who will not have any sense that you are there? Why, as a relative of mine asked me, would we put our son through this grief? Would the morally upright response not have been the certain finality that abortion could provide? No months of agony. No saying "Hello" only to have to say immediately "Good-bye." No chance of a stillborn. No need for a possible funeral or a burial. Abortion would have allegedly provided the certainty of immediate answers to tormenting questions, but it was never a choice for us.

Instead, my wife and I wished very much to hold her and comfort her and speak to her. We wanted our three-year-old son to meet his sister. After the diagnosis, we took each day at a time, taking bittersweet joy in every kick, roll, bend, twist, and turn Vivian made in the womb. We recorded each sonogram and watched intently as Vivian seemed to wave at us or give us a thumbs-up. We cheered her as she practiced breathing. We giggled when she had the hiccups. Vivian was very active in the womb, so active we'd never have guessed she had a fatal condition. The girl hardly slept. And she loved chocolate. When Genece ate chocolate before bed, she ensured that Vivian would keep her awake for a few hours.

Vivian was also very strong. A few weeks before her due date, she pressed out her foot so firmly that I could feel the individual toes and the ridges between them. She was so strong, yet so fragile. We made a decision early on to explain Vivian's condition to our son in terms he might understand. We asked him what he wanted to do with Vivian when she was born. He said he wanted to teach her how to play with garbage trucks.

4

From Faith to Religious Faith

The infancy of my faith did not bear the signs of a religious faith; it was a way I had of keeping my balance while holding on to the fragments of my shattered life—a way of maintaining relationships with my parents amid their separate worlds and conflicting stories. I was initiated into the Catholic Church when my mom reclaimed her faith, and I went along with it as a dutiful son, but I didn't make it my own until after my mom and stepdad moved from California to Iowa, and I found myself thrown into a new setting and new conflicts.

I didn't know what to think when Mom notified me that we would be moving across the country. I knew enough geography to know that I'd be saying good-bye to mountains and beaches, but I was grossly ignorant beyond those details. I informed a few of my fellow fourth graders, and we all concluded that I was leaving civilization for wild plains of flat earth and endless fields of corn. Iowa apparently had more pigs than people, and somehow we got it into our heads that once settled in Iowa, I would have to buy a pig and ride him to school because no one there drove a car. Our family visit cleared up my misconception.

After my mom and stepdad located a suitable church—their first priority—we moved to Ankeny, a suburb north of Des Moines, and I entered the fifth grade at Southeast Elementary, a public school. This move weighed heavily on my shoulders. Instead of seeing my dad on the weekends, I would get to visit him only during the summer. This took a toll on our relationship and drew us apart.

I would fly back to see him twice during the year, each visit lasting six weeks, but the partings and long travels proved too much for me. Like my mom, Dad had remarried; this was complicated because my new stepmom had children already. I felt out of place and uprooted when visiting this family, and my dad and I just weren't close enough to make it work. Toward the end of the second visit, I told him, in tears, that I didn't know if I would be coming back. I didn't return the next year, and I never saw him again.

We spoke on the phone occasionally over the next few years, but the calls became less frequent, and we lost touch. We had almost no contact over the following twenty years and often no current contact information if the mood to pick up the phone did strike us. I seldom gave him much thought, but not out of animosity. We had drifted apart, and my dad steadily became a vague, distant figure from my childhood.

I had a momentary scare once. I received in the mail an offer for commemorative plates that included a letter. It was obscurely written and mentioned something about my father recently passing. At this time, my mom still had his number buried somewhere. She dug it up, I called my dad, and I was relieved when he answered. I was glad to hear his voice sounding alive and well, but we didn't speak again after that for more than a decade.

A few years ago, while checking e-mail, I noticed that my blog had a new follower named Joe Cupp. Shortly after that, I received an e-mail from my dad. We exchanged phone numbers, and I called him. From what I could gather, he was living in some kind of assisted-living home, and his health was not good. We talked for more than an hour, catching each other up on our lives, sharing our joys and heartaches.

Our conversation was warmhearted and pleasant, but I'm ashamed to say I didn't call him again. We exchanged a few e-mails after that, but once again we lost touch.

He passed away in early December of 2012, but I didn't hear of his death until a few weeks later. Mom had learned of his death only after an old acquaintance from her high school sent her a note on Facebook. Mom then called me. I took the news with some sadness, but little surprise. For years I had wondered if my dad still lived, but I had never taken the initiative to find him. When we talked on the phone for the last time, I could hear in his voice the frailty of his age. I enjoyed our conversation, but I had no commanding desire to fly out to see him. To me, he was still a distant figure from mostly forgotten years.

If the distance between Dad and me had already developed before Mom and I moved across the country, then the relocation to Iowa accelerated its growth. Loneliness took hold of me. My stepdad, Patrick, welcomed me as his own, caring for me as a father, but I couldn't respond fully as his son. In California, when he and Mom first got together, I responded gleefully. "Oh, boy! A half dad!" I proclaimed one day. My mom was pleased that I had welcomed Patrick. My father, however, did not approve of my calling Patrick "Dad" and asked me to stop. I obeyed. I withdrew then, feeling far from both my fathers. At that point, a burning emptiness opened up deep in my soul.

Fifth grade found me friendless and socially awkward. Perhaps my nerd credentials had long been on display and I had been oblivious to them. I did not fit in with the other students, and I knew it. Some bullied me. Others ridiculed me from afar. I made a few friends, but I felt bad for them because their friendship with me lowered their already-low social standing. In middle school, the girlfriend of someone I thought was a buddy of mine approached me in the cafeteria. "Phil doesn't want you to hang out with him anymore," she apprised me in the sort of tone you don't argue with. This trend continued through high school, although it dissipated a little with each passing year.

By the grace of God, one friend in particular stuck with me into high school. He was a nondenominational Christian and smart, and he did not look approvingly on my Catholicism. Over the years we debated the meaning of biblical passages and argued about the origins of the church. His biting criticisms and piercing questions had me investigating my faith tradition with more gusto and determination than I'd ever had. I began reading rudimentary theology texts and books on apologetics.

At first, pride motivated my defensive maneuvers; I wanted to be right. But, thanks to my friend, I also fell in love with my faith, and I found within its history and teaching a figure of fatherhood that I desperately needed. God the Father filled my deep emptiness and healed the burns in my soul. Reading the word of God became less about gathering artillery for the battle and more about a relationship with a distant being, a closeness I could perhaps find through prayer, fasting, and worship. Even when I kneeled before the Eucharist, my thoughts passed through the figure of the Son and to the unseen God I wanted to approach metaphorically as my father.

When I needed a father, I found the fatherhood of God. I discovered a person disclosed by the Scriptures I studied and the sacraments I received. I chose to embrace this person as my truest father. I recall the moment I formally made this choice. I was alone on our driveway, shooting hoops poorly, contemplating my God intently. And then I knew who my father was and what I had to do. And so I did it. I called my God "father," not as an abstraction, but as a term of endearment from a son.

This was the time during which my faith transformed into a religious faith. Mass became more important to me. I confessed my sins with more purpose. I spent hours before the Blessed Sacrament. I joined a youth group and went on retreats. I sought to know my God better so that I could love my God better. The metaphorical image of heavenly fatherhood began my relationship with God, but in time I came to approach God by way of other figures as well, masculine and feminine and otherwise.

And so my Catholic faith became more than an exterior setting in which my mom and stepdad had situated me. I internalized it and allowed it to transform me and set the direction my life would take.

The way we imagine God sets the road we will take.

5

Living Eternally Now

With my daughter's looming death, I realized why we frail human beings harvest the faith that nourishes and sustains love. We do so in response to the inevitability of death. I'd long understood how religious faith could give comfort to people nearing their own death or witnessing the imminent death of loved ones, but it wasn't until death became real for me that I grasped the bond between faith and death and saw how my daughter's mortality bid me to have faith so that I could give her my love.

My wife rightly says that I live in the present, and this is true in the way I live my faith. When I say that I have faith, I do not mean that I feel with certitude that there will be life after death. I hope heaven is a literal truth, but I spend little time these days imagining beatific visions or hellish fires. I'm less preoccupied with where I will spend eternity later than with how I live eternally *now*. Do I love? Do I disclose the love of Christ to those I encounter? Do I seek the loving face of God in their imperfect faces? Only on occasion and seldom well, I'm ashamed to say. I fail more often than I succeed. My love falters because my faith sometimes fails.

When my wife's doctor sat us down, I knew I needed grace beyond measure to fuel my heart and give me the strength to love in the face of inevitable, inescapable loss. I would need unbroken faith if I were to love with a broken heart. The theologians tell us that faith is a gift, and with the revelation of Vivian's anencephaly, I began to understand this truth. Whatever I could bring to the table, it would not be enough to sustain me. I didn't have the strength of faith to love into death, but I made a choice—a choice that broke my heart but enabled me to love. I chose to accept the gift of Vivian's life and the gift of faith that her condition asked of me. And in choosing to have faith, even with my flawed and fragile will, I heard a call to love with all my being, passionately and unconditionally, a call to respond to Vivian's life and make it meaningful.

I cannot explain this call. I cannot say for certain where it came from or that it was what I hoped it was—the voice of God. The news about my daughter Vivian called for faith, but it didn't call for certainty. My daughter's approaching death beckoned me to open my heart and give my daughter the love she deserved. When I realized this, my faith experienced its own new birth of sorts, and it was this faith that made it possible for me to enter Vivian's story and be a part of it. By this faith, I approached her departure with the hope that my love would transcend her death, regardless of whether we would meet again. I had certainty of nothing: no surety that Vivian would survive to term; no promise that God would give us the graces for the whole ordeal; no guarantee that God was truly present, suffering with us. I couldn't say why God allowed Vivian to have this condition or whether God had anything to do with it. I lacked the certainty to cast any blame or find a suitable reply to people who congratulated my wife on her pregnancy. I remained in the dark, as if I, too, were in a womb, able to do little more than wait and see.

This darkness of uncertainty is no more visible than in the invisibility of death. Death is the grand uncertainty, "the undiscovered country," in the words of Shakespeare's Hamlet. It's been called the great unknown. I think of it as the *wholly other*. If death is a way of being, then it is a way we can imagine only through figures and metaphors that conceal more than they reveal. In this, death is like God, ineffable otherness. We see death only in the decaying of what remains. The part of us that subsists after death eludes our senses and our knowledge. We can only speculate, wonder, and imagine on the basis of the poetic promises of revelation.

Faith and death are closely connected, and not only because many people of faith believe in some form of afterlife. Faith is a journey in relative darkness, but where does this journey end this side of eternity? It ends in death, which to us is absolute darkness, the supreme unknown. The philosopher Martin Heidegger described human beings as beings-toward-death. We know that we're going to die, that what we are and what we do will come to some kind of end. Death will complete our uncompleted lives.

Simply by living, we move toward death, but faith points us in death's direction, and it calls us to love even when confronted by death's shrouded face. In different ways, both death and love are the reasons for faith. Faith gives us the purpose to love despite our knowing that death will take us and our loved ones. Death separates us from those we love, breaking even insoluble bonds—yet by faith we hope that love is eternal. Faith conquers death by affirming that love is not constrained by time.

For the love of our unborn daughter, Genece did what she could to stay healthy, exercise, and eat well. She made gifts to present to our daughter on her hoped-for day of birth. She felt Vivian roll and kick in the womb, and she savored those precious gifts from Vivian. Prior to this experience, when pondering the meaning of fatherhood, I would have thought of showing my children affection, forming their character, teaching them their parts of speech, instructing them in the faith, or playing games of all sorts. I had been able to do these things and more with my son. Vivian would not likely have the opportunity to see me smile at her, hear my words of affection, or feel me holding her. Anencephaly doesn't generally allow for such sensations.

I came to the conclusion that what it meant to be a father to Vivian was this: I was there with her, suffering with her, even if she could not know me, even if we both were in the dark. Was this experience of fatherhood in any way akin to the fatherhood of God, who loves and weeps for his children? I wonder. God doesn't always get what he wants. In the Christian account, he is our loving Father, not a cosmic engineer who prevents all disasters or fixes all breakdowns in the system. We certainly couldn't fix our daughter's condition. Nor could we have prevented it. Perhaps the same could be said of God. This fatal birth happened as many sad events happen. All I could do was love my daughter and suffer with her, doing my best to be a father to her, and praying for the graces to be a good one.

6

Why I Believe in God

I believe in God because I believe in love. Being a child of loving parents, a brother to my dear siblings, a husband to my beloved Genece, a father to my own lovable and troublemaking children, and a friend to cherished friends has taught me a way of relating to others that transcends desire and knowledge and will. This way is love. It is the movement of one's very being toward others for their sake and for their good. The presence of others calls me to love—family, friends, neighbors, strangers, and even enemies.

My faith in God begins with the simple openness to respond to others in love—in deed and in truth—and without the assurance that my love will bear any fruit. Love means risk and uncertainty. It makes me vulnerable to the tragic, to whatever may come, even to death. Love is an act of faith—*the* act of faith. Love may be returned with rejection or with mockery, with apathy or with scorn, made all the worse because when we love, we remove our armor. Only those who love can be tragically destroyed, but then, only those who love can joyously live.

I count it a blessing, in the truest sense of the word, that I have received love from others. My parents brought me up with care, correction, and devotion. My stepparents embraced me as one of their own. My siblings—Ryan, Scott, Frank, John, Leo, and Faith Ann—taught me to care and what it means to love others more than myself. My friends have welcomed me and aided me in times of need. My wife humors me and pushes me toward my best self. My children insist on daily hugs and kisses, and in showing me in precise detail the drawings they've made and the constructions they've built.

I may be reading too much into my own experiences, but in all of these unique gifts of love, and in the different kinds of love that I give, I sense a sort of unity or presence—a oneness that comes to life in each embodiment of love, even in the most fragmented situations. It's as if love itself has a being, is itself a presence that binds and shines through all instances of charity, affection, agape, romance, hospitality, and friendship. By being in love, I have experienced a *being* of love. I cannot mend the shattered fragments and stories of my life, and yet this being of love has called me to wholeness.

This being speaks, in a voice both silent and awesomely real. It commands and beckons and never shuts up. When I was a child, love demanded that I honor my parents, obeying and respecting them. Love meant that, as a brother, I must share my toys and my space. Love means that, as a husband, I give everything to my wife, uniting my will with hers, forming a family, and consulting with her before I run to the game store to purchase the latest installment of *Final Fantasy*. Love means that, as a father, I experience sleepless nights, the near loss of any "me time," and being a poop coach who is on call 24/7. Love has meant self-emptying and self-giving—what theologians call "kenosis." It is a way of giving all, keeping nothing, and gaining everything. In love, I transcend myself, enter into the being of others, and return creatively to my true self. I empty myself of time and energy and ego, and I discover what it means to be fully human. I become *human* by being a creature of love. This is the logic of my religious faith.

Among the scariest moments in my life were the day of my wedding and the day we left the hospital with our firstborn son, Jonathan. These occasions did not frighten me in a nightmarish sense, but they were terrifying. At these moments I realized, keenly and without obstruction, exactly what love demanded of me as a soon-to-be husband and a new father. Love calls for a response. Before these events, I knew this intellectually, but I did not *really* know it experientially. When we spoke our vows, our lives and selves ceased to be our own. When my wife was wheeled out of the hospital carrying Jonathan in his new car seat, our wants and needs became secondary. No hospital staff would be coming to our home to care for Jonathan while we rested.

In these moments, love—again, love that is its own entity, a being—seemed to speak to me, beckon to me, and demand that I give everything, and warn me of fierce judgment were I to sin against my family and make a mess of things. I was frightened because I didn't feel as though I could respond adequately—a feeling I would probably have more often were I less comfortably complacent in my many relationships.

I do not love as I should. I'm too quick to sit at the computer when I get home, when my wife, son, and daughter Mirielle deserve my attention. I am too eager to leave the dinner table to get started on the evening chores so I can then blog without guilt. Regrettably, I do not give myself to those I love as if today were my last day with them. Perhaps as a consequence, I do not hear the voice of love as loudly as I have at other times. I hear it, but from a distance.

Sometimes, love's voice registers with me too late for my response. When news of my father's death reached me, I did not feel as a son should feel. I was sorry to hear of my father's passing, but I was not full of sorrow. I reacted the way I would upon hearing that the relative of some friend had died. Solemn and sorry, I offered prayers, but no tears. He was too distant, a fragment of my life now too far away. I had figured that I would not see him again and had resigned myself to this. Now I knew. And now I regret. My faith in him and in his fatherhood had diminished over the years, and I had done nothing to keep it alive. I failed him, ultimately. I failed to love him. And now he's gone and I can do nothing but pray, which seems next to nothing, too little and too late, a fool's attempt to undo what cannot be undone.

I fail to love time and again, but when I succeed, I feel more myself than when I focus on my wants and needs. In love, I feel more whole, more vital, and more my true self, as if love builds me up, as if by participating in the being of love I become a full human being. Then my fright fuses with happiness.

My sense of love is a sense of the eternal in time. You may have had the experience of just getting to know someone but feeling as though you've known him or her forever. I have felt this way with some of my friends and with my children, but especially with my wife, Genece, when we share time playing chess, doing dishes, reading books, enjoying each other's silent company, or when I'm alone, thinking of her fondly. I have felt it with my children, as if they've always been with us, as if time opens the door to eternity when I'm practicing taekwondo or playing video games with my son, or when I'm cuddling and dancing with my baby daughter, slowly to the music of Katie Melua or playfully to the melodies of Belle and Sebastian.

Strange as it may sound, by being a son, a father, a husband, and a friend, I have found myself in a loving relationship with love itself, as if love were a person. What I say here is not a certainty, not a proof, but a suspicion—an apprehension of transcendence. For me, this intuition is enough. Come what may, I call this being of love by the name of God. The traditional religions say much more about God, of course, and so do I, but it is here in these modest experiences of loving others and of being loved that my faith is rooted. It is here that I fall when my faith falters, when my antagonistic inner inquisitors get the better of me, when I lose my intellectual hold on the God of the Nicene Creed. When unmoved by the "unmoved Mover" and when unconvinced by the "uncaused Cause," I am lifted by the lowly power of godly love. Because I believe in love, I believe in God.

The first letter of John tells us that God is love. I believe this. My faith begins with this. To love is to recite, in deed and in truth, the most foundational creed. All religious tenets and doctrines worth believing are built with the raw material of love. Without the foundation of love, religion falls to ruin. Without the fruit of love, faith has no purpose worth learning. God is love, and love is of God. The words are inseparable, even if not wholly synonymous.

I believe that anyone who has truly loved another has shown and seen the face of God. God shines in the eyes of a new mother, falls in the tears of mourning children, dances with newlyweds on their wedding day, and is felt in the helping hands that lift you up in your need. All those who love are born of love and know love, and so they are born of God and know God. God is love. The Franciscans like to say that the world is pregnant with God,[2] and that we give birth to God when we love one another.[3]

In love, we abide in God and God abides in us. When we give and receive love, we give and receive God. God is an action one does and a gift one gives and a being one finds. God is a name for what the way of love reveals.

7

The Purpose of Religion

Religion ought to serve love above all else. Following St. Augustine, the philosopher John Caputo defined religion as the love of God, and I agree with this as a basic foundation.[4]

For me, love is religion's true purpose. Religion gives enlightenment, disposition, form, and content to my being in love. Everything religion has to teach me, every myth it composes, every ritual it institutes, every sacrament it offers, should make me a better lover, better at giving and receiving love. *Religious faith*, then, is a way of being in love—of being for others, for their good—that orients me toward the being of love itself, which I call God.

Christians often speak of the day they accepted Christ as their savior. I refer to the day I enthusiastically embraced God as my father and Christ as my brother and the Holy Spirit as the love between them that inspires me. The word *enthusiasm* comes from the Greek *entheos*, which means "in God" or "within God." No greater enthusiasm have I felt than in the passions and inspirations of love.

Since becoming parents over six years ago, my wife and I have not been able to experience the Mass with as much focus as we did in our days before children. Small children cry and fuss, distracting us and others, and so frequently we have to exit to the narthex or hallway. We attended the Easter Vigil when my son was still a baby, and because

Genece was singing in the schola choir, Jonathan had to stay with me. He was not at all pleased, so I didn't even attempt to find a seat in the sanctuary.

For the first part of the Mass, I hid away until he fell asleep in my arms, then I stood in the hallway and narthex, swaying with soft steps to keep him calm and resting. He breathed into my shoulder with that whimper babies make when falling asleep after a long cry. I stood in the hallway where I could hear the prayers and songs of the Mass and follow along. Genece was assigned to sing the alleluia, and as I had hoped, I was able to hear her.

My arms and back ached from holding my very heavy son, but I held him close, absorbing the heat from his head and body, hearing his sad but quieting breath, and listened to my wife sing of her love for God. The moment was awesome in the richest sense of the word. As glorious as my wife sounded, her prayer would not have been as sublime and beautiful and heavenly had I sat alone comfortably in a seat. I felt love wash over me: love for my sleeping son, love for my singing wife, and love for the God whose praises we sang. I felt enthusiastic with love and intimately close to my son, my wife, and my God.

Church is not merely a place to which I go; it is a living and moving body of which I am a member. Places such as my home parish matter to me, but sometimes I have to take the communal practices and enthusiasm of my faith with me on the road. Otherwise, they do me no good. Grace should not be left at the altar, alone to stare at stained-glass windows until the next Sunday. I attend Mass in the hope that my doing so will energize and guide the love that should mark my every thought, feeling, decision, and action. I go to church to learn how to love and for the grace to strengthen and soften my heart. I go there to be a lover here, wherever I am and whatever I'm doing.

Everything religion has to offer should be organized by and ordered toward love. Regrettably, this often is not the case. For my part, I volunteer for ministry proudly seeking affirmation. I pray, wanting my will to be done. I study my faith in preparation for picking fights. When I listen to scriptural readings and sermons, my thoughts turn to those *other people* who really need to hear what is being said. I miss the point. I forget that my way of love cannot survive on the scraps of half-heard homilies or a few moments a week on my knees.

Too often, religion becomes a way of adding high and mighty sanction to my likes and dislikes, passions and hates. It is used to aggrandize the ego—to cloak my will and wishes in divine clothing. My disregard for others becomes a heavenly disposition. My hatred becomes divine wrath. My gut reactions become the eternal law. It's easy to say that these uses of religion pervert real religion, but these are ways in which religion is really practiced. I firmly believe that religion should be ordered toward love, but no religion fulfills this purpose all of the time. No religious person, however holy, strives for it every moment. Religion has its own kind of power that tempts prophets, pastors, and laity alike. Critics of religion spare no expense in dissecting the hypocrisies and corruptions of religious leaders and their faithful followers, and it is good that they do so. Self-serving religion begs for belligerent criticism.

Once when I remarked that religion ought to serve love, a friend of mine, who was no friend to my religion, quipped that I wanted religion to be the opposite of what it is. He was grossly overgeneralizing, but his sentiment bore a truth. We religiously faithful have given religion a bad name and a poisonous reputation. Apostasy today involves more than souls casually falling away from their faith; it features people who have rejected the faith of their parents on moral grounds, who have left in moral revulsion toward perverse beliefs, despicable scandals, and frightful abuses of power.

Speaking of religion as a response to the revelation of God—while I believe true—can lead us to confuse the one with the other, in effect idealizing religion and separating it from the messiness of the human condition. Religion calls believers to seek ideals, but we should not mistake religion for its ideals. Religion includes ideals but also the believers like me who fail to achieve or even reach out for them. Religion gestures toward God, but no religion is a full-time exemplar of godliness. The reality of religion embodies a history of individual and institutional failure and sin. Of course it does. Religion is done by fallen human beings, not pure, spotless gods and goddesses.

It helps me to remember that my religion is a means to an end: loving communion with God and neighbor. This is the purpose of religion. Whenever religion fails to fulfill this purpose, when it becomes about power and not about kenosis, it needs reformation. Whenever I stray from the path of self-emptying love, I need conversion.

8

Loving into Death

I'm told that heaven is the state of supreme, definitive happiness, but I must confess that the concept of a sad God and sadness as part of heavenly experience appeals to me. As a priest friend of mine loves to remind me, I know next to nothing about the finer details of theology, so what I say here should be taken as a poetic musing rather than an attempt to chart a theological or doctrinal course. But we have to image God, don't we? And our images all fall short, whether we imagine God as an almighty king, a Trinity, a suffering servant, a father, a judge, or a lover. The Gospels speak of a weak and humble God, a figure who is betrayed, who serves, who suffers, who weeps, and who dies. My imagining God as sad is hardly novel. Sadness has been a key part of my relatively short life; it defines who I am and who I will be. I no more wish to give up my sadness and the way it has shaped me than I wish to give up my very existence. A sad God makes sense to me, as much sense as any God.

So does a humble God. Sister Ilia Delio, O.S.F., in her book *The Humility of God*, describes God's poverty and humility in terms of love, kenosis, self-emptying.[5] This is a God who descended in love to meet us, who in doing so took on our defects, wounds, and brokenness, a God whom, if I dared, I could find in the disfigurement of my daughter. Vivian, frail and fragile, was pregnant with this humble God, a God who suffered with her and with us.

I have mentioned not being able to assign blame to anyone for our little Vivian's condition. I include God in this. Oddly, for all my dark nights of the soul and never much of a dawn, the problem of resolving God's omnipotence with the evil, suffering, and misery in the world has seldom given me much pause. I understand why people raise the issue, but the conflict, so to speak, doesn't bother me. Anencephaly is like any other disaster. Like the young boy in the film *Magnolia* watching the rainfall of frogs, I can say little more than, "This is something that happens." Did God have anything to do with Vivian's diagnosis? No one can say. I surely cannot. I cannot even say that it was part of God's plan, because God doesn't always get what he wants. God's will is not always realized. There's no comfort for me in confident declarations that God allowed Vivian to suffer so that some good could result, but neither is there a need for me to ask God, "Why?" Perhaps there is no why beyond "this is something that happens."

I don't envision God as indifferent and aloof, watching us from a distance. And I don't deny that God may orchestrate the physical events of the universe according to his will. As a matter of emphasis, however, I imagine God's involvement in the world as an incarnation of love rather than of power. I leave it to others to dust for God's fingerprints on every close call, prayerful decision, natural disaster, and unspeakable crime. If the powerful hands of God smite some people, rescue others, and allow yet others to suffer harm, I am blind to these movements of divine power. If I have sensed God at all, and of this I remain dubious, it has been in the lowliness of existence—in tears, deformities, and hard-fought breaths.

Vivian still seemed to be going strong at the due date. Two weeks later, on the night of September 21, 2009, my wife was induced to begin labor. So close now to meeting Vivian face-to-face, we knew that

Vivian's death was imminent. Night turned to day, day passed into night, night met the dawn, and still we actively waited, my wife especially so. It seemed senseless to pray for a miracle of healing, so I prayed only for a little time after the delivery to be there for Vivian as best we could.

Vivian's approaching death was the end of my faith, not because her death would conquer my faith, but because her impending death was the reason I needed faith. Without an act of faith, I could not offer all my love when her life was agonizingly uncertain and her death so frightfully near. This is why I say that faith, which begins with the openness to love, and which carries us into the very being of others, ends with death. The death of those we love is the end for which we make acts of faith. Thus, faith discloses the eternal nature of love.

Faith doesn't stop at death; it carries our love into the uncertainty of death. I would not cease to love my daughter following her departure. I would remember her and remain devoted to her memory. I cannot say for certain that we shall meet again, but I can say with hope that I love her and that the thought that she has fallen into nothingness gives me no cause to stop loving her. I love her regardless. I love her unconditionally. If death is the final end, I nonetheless love her. I believe in love. I believe my love for Vivian was and is unconstrained by time.

In the early afternoon on the twenty-third of September, after two nights and two mornings at the hospital, Vivian left the warm comforts of the womb for a cold uncertain world. She came out limp and motionless, and none of us was sure of her status.

And then she yelled out her one and only cry.

9

Facing a Revelation

God can seem nowhere these days. If you're a believer, you've probably wondered why God doesn't pop in for a surprise visit so we can all settle the debate about his existence. I've asked God about this.

I'm not talking about the Second Coming here—I don't want the world to end just yet. I'm nowhere near as magnanimous as I will surely be someday, I fondly look forward to daddy-daughter dances, and I only just recently plunged headfirst into George R. R. Martin's enormous fantasy novel series. I've invested too much time in his unfinished world to have it swept away by the real world's end, or his end, or mine. So I drink to our health.

No, my wish here is much more modest. I want Jesus to show up at the Vatican. Take a sacred stroll through Jerusalem. At least make an unannounced appearance on *The Colbert Report*. Look, I'll settle for a talking untamed lion. Whatever the manifestation, just make sure it's on live video, so we can tweet it in real time and Catholicism can be affirmed as the one true faith.

I get no answer. Maybe I haven't set up voice mail. I follow the pope on Twitter, but as of yet he hasn't indicated a revelation from God in the manner the prophets received. He's not hearing otherworldly voices, in other words. Then again, he probably wouldn't tell us if he were.

In the stories told in Genesis, Adam and Eve conversed with God. So did Noah and Moses and many other figures written about in the Old and New Testaments. God has been said to manifest in a literal voice or at least send a messenger with identification and all the right credentials, but you don't hear much about such encounters these days. When you do, it's usually associated with people who do not see the world sanely.

Unless we're talking about the melodies of Bach, I for one have not heard the voice of God. I've never been sure of God speaking to me; nor have I witnessed what I'm willing to call a miracle. No one has introduced himself to me claiming to be the Almighty. I tend not to interpret strange coincidences in my life as the hand of God opening doors and guiding me through them.

Am I in the place God wants me? Am I living according to his plan? Haven't a clue. I cannot wrap my mind around the idea that God has a plan in motion for the ins and outs of my daily life. If he does, I am blind and deaf to it. I marvel at my friends and family who seem able to discern what God wants for them. I wish I had this sight and hearing, but for now I must go on without them. Sometimes this is frustrating.

Many years ago, I came home from my day at high school and handed my mom the latest edition of the school newspaper. I pointed at a student editorial and asked my parents to read it. They did, and they were upset as I expected they would be. The editorial made a few snide remarks about God not coming down to care for the suffering and oppressed. The writer wanted religious believers to shut their mouths about social issues because God isn't real and consequently shouldn't serve as a basis for public policy.

When I was growing up, I had many friends who were not Catholic, some of whom thought ill of my church, but this was, for me, an early exposure to someone who did not take well to any religion. I'd long enjoyed arguing about Scripture with a good friend of mine who was Protestant, but I had no answer for this student. I couldn't point to some Bible passage; he dismissed the whole of religion as stupidity and superstition. I had nothing concrete to show in response, and this nothingness exasperated me.

I have not heard God speak, at least not in a voice I recognized as divine, but I have witnessed what I am tempted to call a revelation of sorts. *Spiritual* strikes me as a suitable name for the experience, but I will go further and call it a religious event. It happened to me during a religious ritual, or more precisely, while I was standing in a line before the ritual began.

When my brother Ryan asked me to be his confirmation sponsor, I felt honored but a little baffled. We were on good terms, as brothers go, but we had never really been close. Our personalities and interests kept us at something of a distance. We were loners inside and outside the family. We didn't hang out together much, and I could be a real ass to him. When we were kids, I'd pester him at the dinner table to the point that he'd react and be sent to his room for time out, and then I would have to sit at the table worried to death that he'd take revenge by breaking one of my toys. Rarely could I slip away to follow him to our room to make sure he was respecting my things. He may have broken a Lego set once, but my anxiety was almost always unfounded, if at times richly deserved.

Once I even launched a snowball at him, knowing full well that a solid shard of ice was packed inside it, because I had put it there, thinking about the projectile and not what would happen if it smacked him in the head. It smacked him in the head. He toppled and I ran inside, yelling to my mom and stepdad that Ryan was hurt.

He was bleeding profusely when they brought him in. Even then I was loath to admit my fault and explain what happened. Guilt poured out of me like blood from my brother's forehead, but I kept silent before my parents. He needed stitches, but he healed well enough.

All this, yet he asked me to sponsor him for a sacrament. This was undeserved, but I welcomed it. Deep down I may have been relieved. Ryan had to suffer my reputation as one of our school system's most infamous nerds, but here he stood inquiringly, wanting to be associated with his older, disreputable brother, desiring a bond for us that we'd never had.

I don't remember anything of the confirmation itself, but I do vividly remember standing in line with Ryan, waiting to enter the church. We both wore sport coat and tie, not at all our customary dress, and we stood patiently and quietly. We were good at being quiet. I found myself staring at him, at his face in particular, in a not-too-awkward kind of way. I realized how much he had changed over the years.

As I observed his countenance—he was staring elsewhere, as if in serious thought—I was struck with a startling sense of unfamiliarity, as if his facial features were at that moment different from how they had been up to that point. His eyes, nose, brow, cheeks, mouth, and chin each seemed suddenly alien and new, as if his visage were a veil that had been lifted to reveal the face of a stranger.

This vision startled and unsettled me. Something radically foreign and unfamiliar had just sucker punched my consciousness.

Who is this brother of mine? I marveled.

I didn't know him. This is what I realized. This is what I saw. The real Ryan was different from the idea I had of him. I sensed that he always would be different, other. It was as if I had just met him for the first time after years of neglecting my responsibility to introduce myself to him and help prepare him to receive the Holy Spirit.

Maybe this was how the apostles felt when they finally recognized their risen savior. They didn't know him at first. In a sense they should have seen him for who he was, but in another sense they could not have perceived him so. Jesus had an infinite inexhaustibility about him. Seeing Ryan in this way was my first inkling of the inexhaustible depths within my brother.

I cannot say what inspired this vision. Perhaps it was the grace of the moment, my waiting to be witness to a sacrament, soon to make sacred promises as his sponsor. Perhaps it was simply my luck to stand and stare in silence. Whatever its cause, I "saw" what cannot be seen, and I wanted to call it the image and likeness of God.

This experience triggered my inner investigator. I wanted to understand it and what it meant. Each religious experience is unique. This was mine, maybe the only one I was going to get. I *had* to cling to it. It wasn't the epiphany of some great truth or the sight of overwhelming beauty or a vision of fundamental goodness. No stone tablets or mystical roses came with it. It could have been the trick of my eyes and my imagination, but it was still real and still powerful and still meaningful. It's no exaggeration to say that this odd vision changed the course of my whole walk of faith.

10

Faces to Faces

What do you see in the faces of those you love? Have you ever really looked?

When I gazed into Ryan's face before his confirmation, I did not expect to be so startled. When my eyes fell on Genece as she learned the news confirming the fate of Francis Estel, I did not expect to be so moved. These visions happened, so to speak, by themselves or by some power unseen, but over the years I have also tried to see this way consciously.

When I was younger, we collected these picture books that seemed at first to be filled with uninteresting patterns of color, but when you stared at an image in a certain way, recognizable shapes would emerge, rising up from the page like opaque three-dimensional shadows. I couldn't get enough of these books. Some images arose for me right away, but others I couldn't get to show no matter how long I let my eyes rest over the seemingly meaningless pattern. Seeing any of them took a degree of practice, and while I developed a knack for making images appear, my technique was not infallible. My eyes would ache before I would give up the chase.

Sometimes, in quiet moments, I will gaze into the faces of those I love, intent on becoming more familiar with the unfamiliar, of observing the otherness in the same faces I see every day. Seeing into the otherness of those I deeply love has likewise taken practice, and like my occasional failures with the picture books, I do not always see anything new or unfamiliar in someone's face.

I try to see in this way as a sort of prayerful reminder not to be complacent. We need to be surprised by our spouses and children and everyone we love and encounter so that we do not take them for granted or think of them only in relation to us and our own world.

It's easy to reduce others in our minds to their function in society or their use to us. The desires for control and comfort are powerful, and not only for would-be rulers. While in high school I got my first job working at a fast-food restaurant, and I pretty quickly got used to being treated like a mere means to an end. Human interaction was never high on any customer's agenda. They all wanted their meal and quickly. Even those who dined in would sit down in the intentionally uncomfortable seats, scarf down whatever version of grease they ordered, and depart as soon as they were full.

I can't say I was any better. To me, customers were numbers on a printout, my coworkers became functions in a chain of action when the rush hit, and new employees were opportunities for amusement. I sent many a lagging newbie out into the lobby to water the plastic plants or down to the basement storage room in search of bags of dehydrated water.

Those of us who'd been around the restaurant a while would take bets on how long the newbie would search the storage shelves for dehydrated water. We'd yell down hints like "It's next to the bags of dehydrated onions" or "Look across the aisle near the cans of steam." Then we'd all laugh. This was the purpose of new employees. We certainly couldn't have them slowing down our service.

Apparently these were common practical jokes. Years later, when a friend of mine and I stopped at a McDonald's for lunch, I told her about my former mischief. During our conversation, a young-looking employee came out among the tables, watering the plants. I got out of my seat and walked over to the greenery he had just watered. The plants were rooted firmly in bleached white rocks. Fake and now wet.

There was an element of good fun in all this, but looking back, I'd say there was also an unwholesome aspect to our practical jokes. We did them as routines and with no care to how the new employees, who were usually younger than we were, would feel at our ridicule and revelry at their expense.

I've been the target of such ridicule myself. I was an exemplary nerd, dweeb, geek, and dork from the moment I first stepped into public school. My social standing throughout the years may have been slightly higher than the kid who made rubber-cement boogers and stuck them up his nose, but one incident of ill-conceived otherness may have earned me the very bottom spot.

My parents, apparently unaware of fashion trends or forgetful of my social status, bought me a pair of horrid multicolored pants. They looked as though the abstract expressionist painter Jackson Pollock, in a psychedelic frenzy, had imbibed all the colors of the rainbow and then vomited all over the fabric. Never one for style, I wore these pants one day to school, a large public school. Wearing MC Hammer pants would have made less of a scene.

I didn't set any new trends that day. Instead, I showed up and gave the student body an unexpected sight. Students who arrived before the morning bell were to go to the gym and sit on the bleachers. I was in band, however, so I had to drop my trumpet off in the music room before taking my seat and chatting with most likely no one. To get to the music room, I had to cross the gym at a diagonal.

When I first entered, the gym was packed with students talking noisily. As I moved into view I felt the room staring at me, but I didn't dare look around. It seemed to me that all the talking suddenly ceased and the gym became silent. And then laughter erupted. I remember the laughter all too well. I closed myself off from the world that day and never wore those pants in public again. When the book of Leviticus forbade the wearing of polyester (19:19), it really should have included those pants in its list of statutes. I felt unwelcomed and out of place—different and not in a good way.

Having been the object of amusement for my classmates, I should have known better than to treat others in kind. Shamefully, I treated others the way I hated being treated: as a thing. I was happy being the one using others instead of being the one used.

Somewhere along the long lines, I developed more of a conscience. It may have been around the time that grocery stores started using the self-service scanning stations, because I took offense at them and have used them only sparingly. Much toil and labor goes into the production of food and getting it to the shelves of the local store; it's odd that I can purchase it without a shred of human contact. Not only odd, but also wrong. With no word to anyone and with no face-to-face meetings and greetings, I come and go unattached to the lives of people who made it possible for my family and me to share a meal. Technology has shattered our stories, and we've all played along.

Encountering others face-to-face, looking into their eyes, and listening to their voices helps bridge the distances in our fragmented lives. This simple disposition returns the personal to our daily encounters with one another, but it calls for the faith that others will open their depths to us and respond in kind. Faith leads us to others in their otherness, so to speak. It takes faith to love others when our love may be rejected or deliver no fruit. It takes faith to see and to respect others as persons. It takes faith to love in the face of death and to hope that death will not rob our love of its worth.

11

Like a Sad, Glorious Song

"That answers my question," our nurse exclaimed, after Vivian, newly born, cried out.

It answered the question wondered by us all. Vivian was alive. For how long, we couldn't know. A priest had been called from the local parish to come administer an emergency baptism, but he had not yet arrived, so I assumed the responsibility. With warm water and fatherly words, I baptized her in the name of the Father, the Son, and the Holy Spirit. Genece held her close to keep her warm and echoed my words in her heart.

Baptizing my daughter was a strange honor for me. Typically the sacrament of baptism is administered by a priest or deacon, but in emergency situations, anyone can baptize. You don't even have to be Christian so long as you intend what the church intends and follow the proper form. This was an honor I would not have asked to receive, and yet I was glad to do it, appreciating that in these terrible circumstances I could bond in this special way with my daughter. I cut the umbilical cord as well, as fathers often do, but the baptism was more meaningful. It was a way that I could be a parent to Vivian—a way that I could express my faith and hope and love for her.

The priest arrived a little later and performed the full rite. I told him that I had baptized her, but also that I was not in my right mind and could not say for sure that I'd done everything correctly. I'm sure one of ours took.

Our parents were present, as were two of Genece's sisters. After dressing Vivian in warm clothes and a special handmade hat, we passed her around to grandmothers and grandfathers, aunts and an uncle, nieces and a nephew, and friends who could be present. A friend of ours who is a professional photographer snapped thousands of pictures. Vivian did not seem to mind being held by multiple people, but she clearly preferred the touch and embrace of her mother. As Genece hugged her, Vivian gripped my finger.

Her face was bruised but beautiful. She was ticklish, especially in her darling little flat feet, and she had a birthmark on her bottom. As I rocked her back and forth, I wondered if, like me, she would have bounced when she walked. When Genece held her, Vivian blew bubbles and made precious baby noises, one that sounded exactly like "Mommy." She cooed and rooted and tried to nurse.

These moments with friends and family were festive and joyous and deeply sad. Life has a power to draw out wisps of heaven from under the bone-breaking weight of tragedy. Our love for Vivian allowed us to laugh. Jonathan showed his sister his toy garbage trucks and instructed her on the finer points of playing with them. Our love was not constrained by time.

After a while, our families gave us time alone with our daughter. When night came, we rested our eyes and cuddled, listening to the calmness of her breathing. My mom took her for a time to keep an eye and ear on her condition. In the very early morning hours, her breathing became more irregular and her heart rate increased. She struggled, but she made no expression of pain or misery. Her look and utterances were like those of an athlete who knows she's nearing the end of her energy, knows she lacks the stamina to see her to her goal, but runs on, determined to give everything.

Neither my wife nor I will ever forget those last moments of Vivian's life as we held her in our arms and wept and consoled her with insufficient words. We knew when we had reached the point of no return. Fifteen hours after her birth, we held Vivian and held our breath as our baby, holding her rosary, breathed her last. Her soul like a wisp left her body; her body relaxed as if in slow motion; and her life concluded like a soft, peaceful end of a sad, glorious song.

12

The Loss of Certainty

One of the perks of studying philosophy is that it really screws up your head, and if you're lucky, your life as well. I was lucky. A good philosophy class will have you endeavoring to give rational justification for your assumptions and questioning the foundations of your worldview. In studying metaphysics, ethics, epistemology, and aesthetics, you come to realize that no one completely agrees with anyone else in any of these fields. Philosophy has a history of some continuity and a hell of a lot of rupture. Show me two scholars devoted to the work of a philosopher and I'll show you where they disagree.

I'm not saying that everyone in philosophy is equally right or equally wrong; nor do I think it impossible to attain any philosophical truth. The point is, no one can write the perennial philosophy. The French hermeneutic philosopher Paul Ricoeur, of whom I am a diehard groupie, said this, and he was right.[6]

There may be nothing new under the sun, but a person can always stand under the sun from a different spot. What others have described you can describe in other ways. Your unique place means that you will see the sun and what's under it from a different perspective from others. You will focus on different things. You'll interpret what you perceive in a way that is uniquely yours. Never seeing the whole, you'll make sense of the parts as best you can from your own place. You study other philosophers to help you expand your place and your horizons so you can see more even if you cannot see all.

Philosophy is grueling work, which explains why I haven't made a career of it. You spend your days poking holes in the presuppositions and arguments of others, and if you're smart like Socrates, in your own as well. Philosophy is the love of wisdom, not the adoration of antagonism. You want to understand, but there's no understanding philosophical truth without engaging the history of philosophy. You can't go it alone. Whether you realize it or not, your ways of thinking were given to you by history. Plato, Aristotle, Kant, and Nietzsche have influenced your thinking whether or not you have actually read them.

After a little kicking and screaming on my part, philosophy showed me how conditional and contingent my grasp of truth really was. I had to let go of assumptions I could not justify beyond shrugging my shoulders. My hold on ideas became much more tentative. I wrote my thesis over six weeks, a fairly brief period, but I was already beginning to abandon some of my premises and conclusions when the defense of it came around. And I had picked a topic I was really opinionated about!

Don't tell anyone, but I started applying this critical suspicion to my religious beliefs. I know that sounds dangerous, but you have to think critically about these matters lest you fall prey to hucksters, charlatans, or postmodern papists like me, who are the worst. As a rule, I'm told to assent to religious truths on the basis of the say-so of some religious authority. That's not a major problem, necessarily—everything I know presupposes some unproven assumption or other—but it is good cause to ask questions. You can expect the Kyle Cupp inquisition. It's what I do.

The first belief of mine that I began to seriously doubt was the notion that my being Catholic meant I had the fullness of truth at my disposal. You see, I took this tenet of the faith to mean that the visible Catholic Church possessed all the religious truth fit to print. I had assumed that this fullness referred to a set of declarations, principles, and arguments—things I could put into a heavy, gold-rimmed book with which to smack heretics and atheists. Beating up sinners had been an important part of my religion. So what happened? I was home for the holidays, having nothing much to do, when it dawned on me that my understanding of how the church had the fullness of truth made no sense given the relativity and subjectivity of human knowledge. The fullness of truth, it turned out, refers to a Person, not a set of propositions.

The Catholic philosopher Gabriel Marcel stressed this distinction between mystery and problem, and it is one Catholics like me do well to remember. For Marcel, a mystery is something unsolvable because I am too immersed and involved within it to attain an objective distance. I cannot see it in its entirety or take hold of it completely.[7]

During the Mass, the priest proclaims "the Mystery of Faith," to which the congregation professes belief in the death, resurrection, and return of Christ Jesus. These creedal statements, declared during the eucharistic liturgy, convey a mystery that words cannot contain, historical events that transcend observable history and rational explanation. We can perceive their meaning only through a glass, darkly, and so our understanding of what they express can never be full or total. This goes for the pope as well. The meaning of the mystery remains always ahead of us. We may pursue it, even enter into it, but we cannot possess it. To do so is to reduce the mystery to a problem, the infinite to the finite, the divine to the human.

Life is full of many such mysteries: love, justice, beauty, and why my son slaps himself on the head. These mysteries defy full explanation. We cannot have the fullness of truth about them, and we cannot be certain, ultimately, that we've uncovered their truth. Fortunately, it's not important that we be certain of them. It's important that we live them.

I had to let go of my possessiveness of truth because I couldn't give unequivocal justification for any truth I held dear. I cannot prove to you that the Christian God exists or that Christ instituted a church or that what I call my religious faith is not at bottom a psychological defense mechanism I'm unconsciously using to deal with my neurosis. I'm not certain of any of these truths. They are matters of faith, and my faith is an uncertain one.

13

A Dark Road

Through falling ash and brutal cold, a starving father and son walk a barren road, scavenging for what sustenance remains hidden in the burned ruins along their path. They must avoid other nearly starved wretches, who, not content to gather canned goods, have taken to theft, murder, and cannibalism. No plants grow, no animals roam, and no birds fly. Death moves, and ash, but little else. Such is the setting of Cormac McCarthy's novel *The Road*, a meditation on, among other themes, the uncertainty at the base of human existence.

Robbed of the securities of civilization and the very possibility of sharing necessities, the man and the boy have to assume that everyone presents a grave threat to life and limb and to whatever items they carry in their cart. The man wisely trusts no one. The boy longs to give aid and comfort to those who seem safe, but he acquiesces to his father. He seems to understand his father's hardness of heart, but he does not share it. The boy has a faith in others that his father has lost. Not even time will tell whether his faith is foolish or a deeper wisdom.

The two walk not toward hope for a civilized life, but toward the next chance, each slimmer than their starving bodies, for prolonging the time before death, a time they cannot say for sure is preferable to life's end. Not even survival can persist as a sure meaning of life. They fear death and yet yearn for it. They despise their lot but cling to life.

All they know is the bond of love that burns between them, a bond that cannot last, not for lack of will, but for lack of life. Death hounds them both, ensuring that one or the other will ultimately walk the road alone. Then both of them will know only cold and emptiness.

Civilization adds a level of certainty or at least predictability to the human condition. McCarthy has robbed his fictional world of any remaining traces of civilization and, in so doing, has highlighted the artificiality and fragility of this certainty. He suggests that uncertainty underlies the human condition, which would mean that all certainty is at bottom relative. *The Road* is exceedingly dark and exceptionally illuminating. The novel embodies better than my words can the real opposition of faith and *certainty*—a truth troubling to many of us.

This is not a mainstream view, by the way. A recent and much publicized survey asked Americans whether they believed in God and asked them to measure that belief on the basis of how certain they were of God's existence. The majority of those surveyed answered that they were "absolutely certain." Other answers included "fairly certain" and "not at all certain." This would have been a poor survey to assess my faith. Nowadays I don't measure the strength of my faith based on the degree of certainty I have. Certainty really has nothing to do with it.

In fact, when I mention in conversations that my religious faith is an *uncertain* faith, I am sometimes met with bewildered expressions, with words of concern, and, especially online, with aggressive push-back from my more feisty respondents. I have been accused by other Catholic Christians of harboring a remarkably weak religiosity, advocating skepticism, misusing words, causing scandal, and advocating mortal sin against the very faith I claim to believe. I disagree with these judgments, but I have to admit, compared to the rhetoric of much mainstream American religion, my walk of faith has a strange way about it.

Those Christian faithful who, like me, speak and write about their faith publicly, typically speak with conviction of the God who is. They strive to show constancy in their core beliefs, certitude in the path they set for themselves and for others. They have the truth, they know it, and they set out to spread the good news.

Some of these voices—loud ones—pop up in my RSS reader by speaking with surety about what God wills, about who is destined for where in the afterlife, and about what an ancient text has to say about everything from appropriate techniques for disciplining children to who's suffering under divine punishment by the latest natural disaster. These self-styled prophets are known for their fiery temperament, not for their introspective doubt. They give the impression that faith and certainty are two sides of the same shiny coin.

Not all Christians live their faith the same way, though, so it's no big deal if I'm different, right? Well, there is a problem, at least for me: the Catholic tradition of which I am a part describes faith as certain. Catholic theologians have argued that the choice to believe must have certainty in order to be faith. This was the view of St. Thomas Aquinas. Catholicism has traditionally defined certitude as the perfection of knowledge and says further that the faith derived from divine authority begets absolute certitude in the mind of the recipient. It also associates the strength of my faith with the degree of my certainty.

From the firm standpoint of Catholic teaching, my uncertain faith appears to stand not on solid ground, or even on shaky ground. Forget building a house on rock or even sand—I'm adrift in a stormy sea, futilely and foolishly trying to form a foundation on violently crashing waves. I'm drowning and don't even know it. Or like the cartoon characters of old, I seem to hover over nothing but air, waiting only for a downward glance before plunging into the abyss. And then—thump!—I will have caused quite a mess.

Have I inadvertently set fire to my interior castle and now wander blindly about, suffocating within clouds of deathly smoke? Am I profoundly confused by my own faith, and do I make matters worse by articulating that confusion in writing? Jesus said that those who follow him will not walk in darkness but will have the light of life. The first letter of John warns us that if we say, "We have fellowship with him," while we continue to walk in darkness, we lie and do not act in truth. Isaiah says that those who walk in darkness and live in the land of gloom have seen a great light, clearly valuing the latter over the former. Poor fool that I am: even the Bible seems to be against me.

Given the pluralism, fragmentation, and uncertainty that mark our contemporary society, some people might accuse me of being too much *of* the world. My faith resembles that of nonreligious young adults who question the foundations of their beliefs, more and more skeptical of the explanations and answers religions have historically given to life's deepest questions. You may wonder, if I've forsaken certainty, then why do I stay committed to my religious heritage and journey?

You may be asking yourself this same question. You may be one of many people questioning their faith, struggling with it, or unsure that faith still provides a pathway to the truth. I sympathize. Some days I feel more kinship with atheists and agnostics than with my fellow Catholics. You may be wondering if your uncertainty will stand in the way of your having true faith. Perhaps you experience certainty, but someone close to you has communicated her doubts and unbelief. You're worried and heartsick, anxious that her faith will dissipate and disappear like bubbles in a shallow spring. Atheism and agnosticism continue to win converts, notably from among people who have lost a sense of certainty about what they once believed. We can't ignore this fact: the loss of certainty often leads to the abandonment of faith.

But this hasn't been the case for me. As I wrote about in the beginning chapters, my faith grew out of shattered stories and shaky conditions. And this uncertain faith is very much at home within both Catholic orthodoxy and traditional Christianity.

It may help if we better understand the many ways in which the word *certainty* has been used in this religious history.

14

Come What May

Catholicism teaches that faith is certain—and more certain than any human knowledge—because it is founded on the very word of God, who cannot lie. We're moved to believe not by the power of our natural reason, but by the revelation of God.

If God is truth itself in some intelligible way, as we Catholics believe, then a deceitful God is a logical impossibility. We can therefore be certain that, if God has spoken, then what God has said is no lie. We can be certain if we have heard God and heard God correctly, that what God has said is unequivocally true. I highlight this word *if* because it is precisely this question of whether or not we have heard God or heard God correctly that we cannot answer with anything closely approaching certainty. Logically, God cannot deceive us, but our eyes and ears surely can. Even consciousness—our fundamental access to the world and its meaning—can lead us astray, delude us, and otherwise play us falsely.

I told you a little about my social outcast status from fifth grade through high school. It's funny that I'm now Facebook friends with people who wouldn't have taken a minute back then to talk to me. I'm more popular now than I ever was. By college I had gotten past much of my social awkwardness, but I still had an inferiority complex that would make pond scum blush with shame. And, as is often the case with low self-esteem, I compensated by developing narcissistic traits.

For instance, one evening in college, I ran into a friend who was not at that moment particularly friendly to me. She brushed me off with a curt word, and we went our separate ways. I had a little crush on her, so you can imagine that I obsessed over this. I figured I must have done something to upset or offend her. Anger rose in my gut, and I decided I would give her the silent treatment the next time I saw her. The next time I saw her, she was warm and cheerful, but I stuck with my plan, too deluded and self-absorbed to realize that her earlier harsh attitude had nothing to do with me.

I calmed down later and assured myself that her curtness probably had to do with something in her life. I heard her words correctly, but I misinterpreted them wildly. I can do this with God as well. And I have. I've spent more hours than I care to admit before the Blessed Sacrament silently yelling obscenities at God because all my romantic loves were unrequited. I didn't know what God was up to, but I didn't approve of it, whatever it was. I blamed him for not bringing me true love according to my desires and timetable. I felt that God was letting me down or simply playing with me.

When I came to my senses, I reminded myself that the God I believed in and loved was not a sadistic monster. My faith didn't require that I understand the ways of God. Faith implies that I intellectually assent to a belief, but faith does not give me complete and certain understanding of that belief. Faith involves the belief in and assent to things unseen and uncertain. Traditional Catholic thought defines certainty of faith as a choice, not as the possession of knowledge. Faith is certain when I give it, come what may, holding nothing back.

When Genece and I kneeled before the altar saying our wedding vows, we did not know for sure how our life together would turn out. Neither of us had certainty about the fidelity we would give. I had even questioned my feelings a few weeks beforehand, because being in love with Genece didn't feel the same as the intense loves I had felt before. This love didn't hurt, and it took a while for me to realize that what was missing was the pain.

Married couples have to trust themselves and each other precisely because they cannot know what may come to challenge them. This trust—this act of faith—will have to continue, even after the evidence of true love accumulates. Signs of love can be faked. Spouses can deceive one another and themselves. The soul remains a mystery, even to the most penetrating of psychological techniques. One can never be certain, but this is no mark against marital fidelity. In marriage, I choose to have faith in my wife, not in a lifelong status of certainty.

The certainty associated with faith is about my choice to have faith; it's not about how well I grasp, intellectually, what I believe. I don't need certain sight and understanding to have faith in others or in God.

Faith seeks understanding; faith is not the same as my confidence that I understand what I profess to believe. Religious faith is my response to a God who reveals through ambiguous signs and wonders. Religious faith is not the same as being certain that I have heard and understood that revelation.

Faith doesn't allow the faithful to see beyond death or into the unknowable. It is the constancy and steadfastness of the soul to seek the good and the true. The certainty of faith does not bulldoze away the mountains of all difficulties or clear a sure, clean path from the mind to the reality outside it. Faith propels us forward, over and under mountains, within the clouds of unknowing. Those gifted with faith must still, with Socrates, say, "I know that I do not know."

In the sixth installment of the *Final Fantasy* video-game series, the heroes fail to stop the divinity-seeking villain from initiating a cataclysm that will destroy most of the planet but give him unassailable magic power. This self-deification through magical destruction is a motif common to the series and one of the reasons I dig the games so much. In this story, the bad guy succeeds, at least for a time.

After the world is plunged into ruin, one of the characters, the villain-turned-hero Celes, awakes on a small island. She has been unconscious for a year, alive because the one other person on the island has cared for her. He has grown ill and soon perishes. Celes, in despair, throws herself off a precipice into the sea, but she washes up on shore, alive. A bird welcomes her when she awakes on the beach. It has a wound wrapped in a bandana, the kind worn by Locke, one of the other heroes. Celes takes this as a sign that her friends may be alive and searches for a way off the island. When she departs on a raft, she does not know whether or not her friends or anyone remains living, but she sets out believing they survived and determined to reunite with them. This is the kind of uncertain faith I'm trying to describe.

Mine is also a religious faith, but that quality doesn't take away its uncertainty. During the liturgy, I recite creeds and assent to doctrines, not with unquestionable knowledge that they correspond to reality, but with the trust that these statements of belief disclose an unseen world, a trust made possible because I believe in *a person* who has spoken them. This person is Jesus Christ, the Word of God. I trust God's word because I trust in the Word of God and in the witnesses to that Incarnate Word.

So, when I say that I profess an uncertain faith, it's not the same as saying I cannot choose to believe with lasting confidence and full commitment. I do choose, with confidence and commitment, to believe, and my principle beliefs have certain logical consequences. In other words, those beliefs, though uncertain, determine my life's course, and they form me, influencing my attitudes, actions, and inclinations. However, I admit that my mind and senses are fallible and sometimes flawed. I have deceived myself too often to stake my faith on something as unreliable as certainty.

15

The Last Word

It is a wonder that anyone becomes a parent. The possibilities that life will rip out your heart are gruelingly endless. Children fall down, skin knees, and break bones. They get sick and keep you awake all night with worry. You're responsible for the health of their bodies and their souls, and your power is limited and ever dwindling. Whatever path you set for their lives, they will stray. They will make mistakes and succumb to influences from which you would rather protect them.

While cleaning the house recently, we had children's songs playing online via Spotify to keep Jonathan and Mirielle entertained while we all worked. My wife and I tend to tune out the commercial breaks, but we both raised our heads when we heard an advertisement for Trojan condoms. We had hoped that Jonathan had not overheard the catchy lyrics to the commercial's tune, but, when he later belted out "Trojan Man!" while playing with one of his toys, we knew the damage had been done. This was one of those moments of being a parent when you have to act immediately but without creating a disturbance or scene your child will remember. I sat the boy down and we had the talk. Now, years earlier than I would have preferred, he knows all about *The Iliad.*

I dread the days my son and daughter become teenagers. My plan so far has been to corrupt them myself so that when they become rebellious youths, they'll fall into the habit of being upstanding citizens. If this works, I'll have to write another book.

I loved the moments when my son and I would follow the garbage truck around our apartment complex, watching it raise and dump the huge containers. Jonathan would stare wide eyed but snuggle up under my chin and inform me that the noise was not too loud for him. Children fill you with awe by finding everything interesting, even their poop. I had a hard time convincing the boy that his mother did not want to come to the potty and see his business.

"But she might come in here, see my poop, and say, 'Wow, that's so cool!'" he insisted.

Parenthood is an endless state of suspense. I hope my son and daughter will love me always, but I cannot see the future. I don't know what will happen. I don't see us drifting apart as my father and I did, but God only knows what paths we will all take in the end.

I cannot live in the unknown future. I have to live now. I have to love my children now and be thankful for them now. It is a strange grace that their lives would not exist if their siblings had lived. If Francis had come to term, Jonathan would not have been conceived. Had Vivian not left us early, Mirielle would not have arrived. At the present, death does not have the last word. Life and love continue.

16

An Antagonistic Disposition

I vaguely remember being a young child returning to the townhome my mother was renting shortly after the divorce. I sensed that something was very wrong upon walking through the front door. My mother's visible anxiety told me something was amiss before she explained to me why her bedroom closet and dresser were an unexpected mess.

A burglar had broken into our home while we were away and stolen jewelry that had belonged to my mother and her parents before her. Shelves were pulled out, items were tossed about, and the window to her bedroom had been opened but not forced. The sheriff figured the intruder had probably entered and exited from the front door, which was ajar when my mother arrived home from work. He likely had a key, and it was possible that he could return.

I don't recall being overly frightened by the scene—my mother's room looked much like mine after I had made a mess of it—but her demeanor, a mixture of dread and panic, made a strong impression on me. An intruder had entered our home, walked about the place, touched our things, and left with some of them. He was gone, but the place remembered him: the drawers he had touched, the air he had breathed, the bedsheets he had disturbed. This thief had robbed our home of peace and left us with discordance and fear. We did not live there for too much longer.

Like such a thief or someone worse, ideas can intrude into our heads, disturb our interior life, and make a mess of us. Otherness is not always good. Philosophy is no harmless pursuit. Bad ideas often precede vicious deeds. It matters how we think about human nature, our relationships, our political and economic structures, the beautiful and the ugly, and what it means to be moral. Bad philosophy and bad religion have a lot of blood on their hands.

A cautious and critical approach is more than prudent when we expose ourselves to new ideas or untested ways of thinking. Ideologues manipulate the schooled and unschooled alike. Christianity, being concerned with matters of eternal life and death, has historically been very mindful of this. Abandonment and detachment mark much of Christian spirituality. St. Paul urged the Romans not to conform themselves to the age. The first letter of John exhorts its audience not to love the world or the things of the world. In the Gospel of John, Jesus tells his followers that they are not of the world and that the world will hate them. In the spirit of these Scriptures, Christians often speak of the world antagonistically.

It makes sense to be on guard against the world, but this isn't the whole story. The Scriptures also speak of God making the world and deeming it good, of Christ coming into the world by becoming a part of the world, sharing in its nature and making it anew. In this sense, Christians ought very much to be of the world, and not just in it for a time as if we don't belong here. We are not usability testers for the beta version of the universe: our world is the real deal, the outpouring of God's love, the place where the drama of life happens.

Late in my senior year of college, I returned to my dorm with a newly purchased VHS copy of Paul Thomas Anderson's *Magnolia*. I passed through the common room on my way to the stairs. A fellow student, watching the television with some others, noticed what film I had in hand.

"That movie is horrible," she warned me. Her tone indicated that she was not speaking aesthetically, but morally, and that I would be risking sin not to heed her advice.

"You think so? It's my favorite movie," I said, risking a little instigation.

Though *Magnolia* is not as polished as Anderson's *There Will Be Blood* or *The Master*, I still think it the best cinematic display of the human longing for atonement. *Magnolia* is a work by a fallen-away Catholic struggling with themes of sin and grace, despair and hope, guilt and reconciliation, absurdity and providence. It may be a better work of art because of Anderson's uncertainty. He depicts characters without pontificating or telling you exactly how you should feel about their characters' decisions. His care is with the drama of human action and its consequences, with the incarnational and not with the abstract.

Toward the end of the film, two of the more sympathetic but deeply wounded characters, Claudia and Jim, are on a date, which you, if you're like me, hope will go well for them. The dinner becomes instead an occasion for brutal honesty, a scene that becomes difficult to bear for them and for us. Claudia has troubles: drug addiction and an abusive father who's come back into her life. She cautions Jim that he shouldn't want to be with her. Jim says that he'll stay with her whatever her problems are and that she won't scare him away.

Jim, a police officer, had met Claudia earlier that day when he came to her residence after a report of a disturbance. In a breach of ethics, he had asked her out on a date. She accepted, perhaps only to get an officer of the law away from her home in which she had frantically hidden away her drugs. Or perhaps she was lonely or was attracted to a date that was somewhat illegal.

After Claudia's warnings, Jim opens up about his being a laughing-stock on the force for having lost his gun that afternoon. She seems pleased with his honesty but then excuses herself to go to the restroom. When she returns, she asks Jim if, now that he's met her, he would object to never seeing her again. He's aghast, but refuses to say no, even though Claudia begs him to say so before she runs out of the restaurant.

These are tense and honest scenes, difficult but rewarding to watch. Other scenes in the film I cannot discuss in polite company. *Magnolia* is very deserving of its R rating. I don't recommend it to everyone, but I'm not going to shy away from it for this reason or because Paul Thomas Anderson and I disagree about the finer points of theology.

Still, the admonishment I received in the common room came as no surprise. *Magnolia* was not the sort of movie students at this small Catholic school would hasten to see, and I made no attempt to hide it as I passed in clear sight of my fellow students. I walked right into the warning.

In her own day, the author Flannery O'Connor complained of fellow Catholics who mistook an honest representation of sin for sin itself or who insisted that good art needed explicit Christian content. Not much has changed, I'm afraid. I know of a Catholic who refused to go see *The Lord of the Rings* movies because the books had no explicit Christian imagery or thematic content. Dare I say this attitude is antagonism to the world run amok? To quote Harry Potter, yes, I dare.

I'm fairly immersed in the trends of popular culture, and I certainly see the advocacy of principles I do not share and the rejection of principles I hold. But I don't see much in the way of hatred for truth. Our pop culture celebrates too much stupidity and makes a lot of mistakes about the human condition, but I'll always take secular struggles with mystery and manners over didactic piety that claims to have all the answers.

17

A Word I Love

In my senior year at Franciscan University of Steubenville, having nearly completed the core requirements of my studies in English composition and literature, I took a few courses in philosophy to fill in my schedule. I found the field delightful but also humbling.

Writing a paper for a philosophy class demands a different structure and style than crafting papers as an English major. I had a firm grasp of the written word, but I tried to accomplish too much in my first Introduction to Philosophy paper and suffered the consequences. When the professor handed me back my essay marked with a C, I sat there dumbfounded and in disbelief. I was a senior who regularly achieved an A on papers of all sorts. How in Hamlet's rotten Denmark could I have failed so shamefully in a freshman course?

Apparently philosophy professors expected rigid philosophical argumentation in a manner fitting the assignment. I had written what amounted to five papers crammed into one, and so I had not given the due attentiveness to the one paper I was supposed to have written. I deserved the C. It took me a few days to appreciate this truth, but I eventually got it, helped by my mad infatuation with the subject matter.

When I graduated, I had four philosophy classes under my belt. Not having any solid plans for my future, but a boatload of student loan debt, I decided what better way to accrue even more burdensome debt than by going after a master's in philosophy? So I did.

I attended academic presentations and conferences during those next two years. Several made strong impressions on me, but I'd like to tell you about one in particular.

I don't remember the presenter's name, but I recall the setting fairly well. We were gathered in a gallery on campus, two stories high, with stairs to a walkway along the edges of the room. Artwork adorned the walls above and below. Students and faculty from both the philosophy and theology departments sat in chairs that had been placed for the occasion, and we faced the presenter, a chipper fellow whose demeanor alone spoke to you of the love of wisdom. He smiled throughout the evening, during his talk, and even during the Q&A when a professor dismissed the whole of his philosophical project as a reaction to bad Thomism. Here was an individual who exuded the passion that comes from doing well what you love doing.

His presentation was on the Jewish philosopher Emmanuel Levinas, a name I'd heard mentioned but never formally investigated. I learned that evening that Levinas had devoted much philosophical care to a study of the human face and the "otherness" it reveals. Hearing this, I nearly jumped out of my seat. Did this scholar describe the uncanny experience I'd had of looking into my brother's face?

To an extent, he did; he and I would not agree on every point, but we did share a general, powerful idea. Levinas was an early philosopher of alterity. *Alterity* is not a word you hear every day, but I wish it were.[8]

I say it as often as possible and teach it to my children when they first begin to speak. My sister-in-law once dared me on Facebook to go a day without saying the word, and I failed. It is my very favorite word for both its sound and its meaning.

Alterity is the name I give to what I experience when I see into the familiar faces of those I love, enter into their unfamiliarity, and allow their depths to overwhelm my soul. It is what sucker punched my consciousness when Ryan suddenly appeared alien to me. It is the beating heart of hope I heard behind Genece's grieving countenance. When we left the doctor's office that day, no doubt other patients and strangers we passed noticed our sorrow. To them, my wife's appearance would have conveyed despondency—the absence of hope. I had seen something more, something behind the surface.

Alterity means "otherness," but it is most often used to indicate radical otherness or the wholly other. To me it identifies a liminal experience—an in-between or transitional state between knowing and not knowing, between familiarity and unfamiliarity. I've encountered alterity in the flesh only with people I know very well. When I'm riding my bicycle to work and pass neighbors out for a run or parents walking their children to school, I see mostly the unfamiliar faces of strangers. None of these faces has shaken me from my thoughts or disrupted the course and order of my life.

Waiting with my brother before his confirmation, I seemed to stand before the threshold of my brother's very being, and looking in, I apprehended not the young man I knew, but, through his familiar features, a vague, distant trace of his otherness, a sensation that called for reverence just as much as the confirmation Mass did. The hope that shined through my wife's grief likewise called for reverence. I had sat quietly, trying to be strong, but I was also in awe, holding her hand as her sorrow and hope consumed me.

Levinas and the other philosophers of alterity gave me a name for these sorts of experiences. They gave me a name for a direction my faith had already begun to go, and their heavy lifting built a road on which I would come to travel purposefully.

18

God's Otherness Revealed to Us

Jesus put alterity into practice by emphasizing the moral importance of our dispositions toward others. He taught us that our dispositions and attitudes and desires can be sinful. You don't have to literally kill an innocent person to commit murder. Lust itself constitutes adultery in the heart.

This focus on the interior confused me as an adolescent. By the time I was old enough to begin to understand what Jesus was saying, my hormones were out of control, and I fell constantly to lusts of various sorts. I wasn't really old enough to date anyone yet, but I noticed girls. And how! As John Cusack says in *High Fidelity*, they were everywhere. And boy did I enjoy looking everywhere for them.

Deciding one day to show off my newly acquired understanding of this teaching and its seriousness, I confessed to a priest that I had committed adultery. He eyed me gravely and with a twinkle of bewilderment. No screen separated us, you see.

"Are you going to see this person again?" he asked, very seriously.

"Uh, yes," I answered, not comprehending his full meaning.

The priest pressed me further, and after a few more questions, ascertained that I had not in fact committed adultery. I felt foolish and wisely decided then and there not to show off again while confessing my sins—not that I kept that resolution.

I've not had to confess an extramarital affair, but I did make the mistake recently of asking my wife, out of the blue, "Did I ever tell you the story of when I confessed to committing adultery?"

"No," she said, elongating the syllable.

I really must be more careful with how I phrase things. Jesus confused his audience as well, but not from want of careful speaking. He had a better excuse.

Jesus is the embodiment of absolute alterity: to know Jesus is to know the Father. To relate to Jesus—to be in a relationship with him—is to experience the Supreme Other, so to speak. Alterity is a name for God because God is almost wholly other. I say almost because I believe that God has revealed his divinity to us, if in finite expressions. If God were wholly other, then we could not know God at all, not even by way of analogy or negation. Being infinite, though, means that God is infinitely otherwise than the finite ideas we fashion.

The encounter with God is *the* liminal experience of alterity. It is when I sense my belief most clearly that I am most prone to ask God to help my unbelief. The closer I appear to approach God in a relationship, the more distant from God I feel. The more reverently immersed I get into the rituals and sacraments of my religious faith—those ways of giving shape, color, and texture to the countenance of God—the more alien and unrecognizable God seems to me. The categories of "theist" and "atheist" don't do justice to the ambiguity and complexity of my religious experience. They leave out the unbelief that invades my belief and the belief that unexpectedly visits my unbelief.

If alterity is an aspect of God and of every person, then living by faith means hospitality to those we encounter—especially to their unseen depths. It means keeping the doors to our mind and heart open to the presence of others, a presence that may challenge our notions and call us to respond in ways we aren't expecting and for which we are unprepared.

Perhaps no story better illustrates this affirmation of alterity than Mary's yes to the angel Gabriel. When the angel appeared to her, bringing tidings of God's favor and news of an impossible conception, Mary was greatly troubled and asked how this could be. Gabriel's answer was no less obscure and unfathomable—no less words of alterity—but Mary responded in hospitality to this impossible, otherworldly visitation, saying, "Let it be to me." She could not know or explain or understand what this "it" was, but she welcomed it freely, faithfully, and lovingly.

Theologians would later try to make sense of this visitation, defining its terms within a system of thought—downplaying its alterity in favor of intelligibility—but I think Mary gave the better and more appropriate response. After her inquiring "How can this be?" was answered with an equally inexplicable explanation, she chose to act in the only way that could pierce the cloud of unknowing. She answered her own "How can it be?" with "Let it be." She responded in loving service and reverence to her God.

19

The Final Good-Bye

At seven months into the pregnancy, with Vivian kicking in her belly, Genece and I went to the funeral home to pick out a casket and make arrangements for the funeral. I knew the staff, having in my job at the church worked with them before on funerals for others. By then, I had many times been brought into the lives of people during moments of crisis, personal tragedy, turmoil, and loss. Both day and night I received calls with the word that someone had died or was deathly ill.

I knew that Vivian's death would shatter my world and leave me broken and incomplete, but I didn't really know it, not fully, not yet. I had shared words with people preparing to say the final good-bye, but I was not ready to say those words myself.

My wife and I filled out the necessary paperwork, looked at the small baby-sized caskets, and picked out a location in "Baby Land" for Vivian's eventual burial. Then, in a daze, we walked out of the building, returned to our car, and drove home. Vivian kicked throughout the visit, unaware of what we were planning.

Now, but a few weeks later, the time had come. Only the entry light shone in the hospital room, leaving most of the room in darkness. Vivian was still but for the rocking in our arms. We heard a knock on the door and my mom entered. She saw us in tears and she knew.

Neither Genece nor I wanted the funeral home to come and take our daughter away. We held on to her for a while longer, but then it was time to say good-bye. We let her go and we left the hospital and we drove home.

We saw Vivian again when we came to the funeral home to put her in her final dress. I fell apart and sank into a chair and felt every pain ever inflicted on me. At the visitation and the funeral Mass I would keep it together, but here I wept openly and screamed inwardly.

Her funeral Mass was lovely and well attended by friends and family. Afterward, we drove to the cemetery behind the church and laid her to rest. We said our final good-byes.

I used to think a lot about an afterlife, imagining judgments, reunions, and beatific visions. Since the passing of my girl, I reflect less on the hereafter and more on the moment of death itself. I say words to my deceased daughter, often reciting a prayer I wrote for her, and I picture her hearing me. But usually, when my thoughts turn to her, I recall and relive the hours she shared with us.

Memory and grief have become my expressions of faith, as I seem to have mostly abandoned the habit of imagining some future heavenly hope. Consequently, faith has ceased to be a comfort to me. Death has re-created my faith; my heart tells me to remember and to remain in love, to love into death, not because all will ultimately be well, but because a life, though lost, deserves devotion.

My wife and I are broken and will remain broken, but our hearts are, we hope, full of love, and we will hope and strive to keep our faith alive. Our love for Vivian and her love for us was not constrained by time, nor is it now, nor will it ever be. Our love knows no time constraints. Indeed, our love knows eternity, and because our love knows eternity, our love overcomes death.

20

Farewell to Explanation

In the course of my life, I have stated various reasons for my believing in God. Some I've kept; others I have left along the road. Chief among those discarded reasons now collecting dust is what I call *faith as explanation*. I believe in God, but not because the idea of God satisfactorily explains anything about the world.

My son has been able to point out Jesus on our church's San Damiano cross since he was a baby, but it has never served as an answer to his many questions of "Why?" It is an image we teach him to internalize and emulate, not in its violence, of course, but in its love. He's picked up on this message, aided by Luke Skywalker's example. We regularly hear him at play with his action figures, having the good guys offer the bad guys a second chance to become good guys again. Point, Mommy and Daddy. Then again, he's also used the image to defend his disobedience. "I can't take a bath, Daddy," he told me once. "I'm Jesus and I'm stuck on the cross!"

Before we had any children, we used to frequent the stations of the cross. I enjoy the prayer especially because it has motion and a story to it, but our rambunctious little half-pints make entry into its mysterious habit of being nearly impossible for us. The stations are a wonderful exercise and meditation on the meaning of the passion, but they do not *explain* the carrying of the cross or the Crucifixion. These are inexplicable events.

It is worthwhile to speculate on why there is something rather than nothing, but positing a Creator only restates the question. Saying that God created the universe from nothing, bringing space and time into being, is a fancy way of saying that I do not know how the universe came to be. I can only begin to fathom what creation from nothing means, and I can get only so far as my metaphors can take me. If my finite words touch the infinite meaning of God, I cannot know how this happens. I cannot explain it or draw it on a map. The affairs of God are inexplicable. To speak too crudely, God is much too big to serve as an explanation for anything.

The belief that God brought the universe into being through a creative and loving act—a belief I share—may disclose something of who God is, but it cannot serve the function of a scientific or historical explanation of the cosmos. I cannot really explain what "Creator" means, certainly not when I'm applying a human construct to an infinite and divine transcendence. To interpret the creation stories in Genesis or in any other sacred text as explanations mistakes their religious meaning and risks condemning religious faith to an early death.

As atheists are fond of noting—and rightly so!—human history has seen supernatural explanations give way to natural ones, but not the reverse. If I believe in God because positing God seems to answer this, that, and the other thing, then I may have a belief that's not long for this world. A faith that serves explanation will retain its power only so long as explanations are needed. As neurologists, biologists, psychologists, astronomers, and others answer our questions with their findings, a faith that merely serves as explanation will have less and less to say.

21

The Cloud of Unknowing

I wish I could see into the "undiscovered country," that term used by Shakespeare's Hamlet to describe death. I wish I had before me incontrovertible evidence of the existence of God, heaven, and the communion of saints. I don't like to be in the dark, unclear on what's to come. In my own struggles, I deplore waiting for resolution. I want to know what's going on and how everything will eventually play out, unless, that is, we're talking about *The Walking Dead* or any other story spoilers, in which case, hush!

Whenever I had a crush on someone, the worst anxiety accompanied my not knowing if she returned my affection. When, as was inevitably the case, she enlightened me on the absence of her feelings, my yearning would dissipate with relative quickness. The clarification of unrequited love gave me the purpose to move on to another infatuation.

I do understand why people desire certain knowledge. I sympathize with it and desire it myself.

Nevertheless, in the domain of my religious faith, I prefer to cast certainty into the outer darkness. But first, maybe I should define what I am rejecting. I reject the unwillingness to allow that there may be truth beyond what I know or think I know. This kind of thinking is especially dangerous in the spiritual realm because the spiritual is unseen and ultimately ineffable—otherness is its essential feature.

A famous work of fourteenth-century Christian mysticism argued that a "cloud of unknowing" stops all those who reach out for God from seeing him in the clear light of rational understanding. To the intellect, God is forever unknowable, forever unseen except within this cloud. Rational understanding cannot pierce this darkness, so the mind cannot achieve clear sight of what lies beyond. The author of *The Cloud of Unknowing*, whose identity we fittingly do not know, taught that no one will have an unclouded vision of God in this life.[9]

Only by blind, outreaching love can we know God.

If I am to know God, then I must in love and through love reach out to God in the cloud of unknowing, focusing ultimately not on any image of God, but blindly groping for the naked being of God himself. This pursuit of intimacy with God is no mere work of the mind, neither of reason nor of imagination. It is the work of love enthused by the gift of grace.

In our proudly intellectual age, we've forgotten that, through history, religion has involved both reason and ritual. Religions have doctrines and tenets and the like, but they also have myths and liturgies and other ways of being-in-the-world. Christians are supposed to learn the Gospel *so that we can live it.* The story of the Incarnation is meant to be uniquely incarnated in every life. Its purpose is not intellectual certainty, but loving action and, through love, a relationship with God. Like any work of literature, the Gospels call for interpretation, but unlike typical literary works of art, they can be understood only by being retold again in a person's own life. Our beloved Gospels make religious sense only when brought to life by being religiously lived.

The Catholic Mass, for example, incorporates biblical stories into the two liturgies: that of the Word and that of the Eucharist. The Mass incarnates these stories, and at its conclusion, the priest sends us out into the world to embody what we have received into our individual lives. We are to love, and we are to serve. The objectives of this Christian faith are love and service, not unquestionable knowledge about how many days God spent creating the cosmos or what the Holy Spirit really looked like when descending on the apostles. We faithful are sent into the uncertain messiness of the world as lovers and servants, especially to "the least," not to our homes where we can recline and rest in the comfort that we have the fullness of truth.

We cannot know God as we know our family and friends, or the places we've lived, or the ideas we've long pondered. Our knowledge will always fall short of God by an infinite distance. God is other than what we think and leaves behind even the word *other*. A cloud of unknowing separates us from God. Creeds, doctrines, and other formulas do not produce certainty in the mind; they are at best acts of faith, hope, and love. Certainty is not counted among these theological virtues, nor is it the fruit that they bear.

Uncertainty also rules over many of the finite realities before us. Psychologists have shown how even very thoughtful, introspective people can be in error about their own core motivations. I want to assume that I make free, informed decisions and am in control of my own thoughts, feelings, and actions. The possibility that I am not myself, that factors buried deep in my subconscious compel me to act, and that I am, if only in part, unwittingly enslaved to my passions or appetites or old traumas, does not sit well with me. I want to believe that my ideas, emotions, and choices are really mine, but look at how my faith began. You could read my faith origin as an unconscious defense mechanism. I cannot prove to you otherwise.

Sometimes the reality that we remember and believe motivates us isn't actually real. In college, a surreal time in my life if there ever was one, I spent an inordinate amount of time before my little television set, the controller to my PlayStation in hand. One game I never tired of playing and replaying dealt with themes of false memory and motivation.

In the video game *Vagrant Story*, you play a medieval secret agent type who's sent by the government to apprehend a charismatic cult leader after the latter kidnapped a duke's family for unknown reasons. The two men play a cat-and-mouse game through an abandoned city destroyed years previously by a magical earthquake. The cult leader, who seems to have an eerie ability to see into someone's soul, taunts the agent by challenging his memories. Ashley, the agent, witnessed his wife and child's murder, or so he remembers. Sydney, the cult leader and sorcerer, suggests to him that he was not the surviving victim, but the murderer himself, whose memories have been manipulated and altered by the government to mold him into an effective pawn. The story hints at both possibilities but refrains from answering definitively one way or the other.

Now, for the record, I don't believe the government has modified my memories. Nonetheless, as I get older, memories fade, and with these vanishings, my self-knowledge becomes more elusive. When I become indignant or anxious or ill, I do not feel myself, and I catch myself doing and saying things I would ordinarily not say and do. I can't pinpoint where my bodily chemistry ends and my free will begins. Contemplatives spend years in deep introspection, and they still can make only so much progress.

When I reflect on my religious faith and ask myself whether or not I really have that faith, I can't give an answer that is completely true or reliable. I hope that what I call my faith is really my responding to a God who has been revealed, but I cannot prove this to be true beyond a shadow of a doubt. The light of truth may shine without my really standing within it. I may believe not in God, but in a fabrication of my subconscious desires. I may yearn not for truth, but for comfort. The dread of death may compel me. Neurosis may navigate the flight of my soul. Events in my early childhood pretty clearly shaped the faith I have today. Not only is my faith uncertain, I am uncertain about whether or not I even have faith. And that is OK. I believe that I believe, and I ask God to help my unbelief.

"My cuddles have lots of hugs in them," our son Jonathan informed us once. At her bedtime, my daughter Mirielle will usually come to me for a good-night hug and kiss. This is part of her routine, and she wants it to be. My children love me. I harbor no doubts about this, even when the boy explodes in a Sartrean tantrum, madly telling us that he wishes nothing existed, even God. Sure, I'm a little disconcerted when he says he wants to be Batman when he grows up but questions me with "Why?" when I tell him he should have a different origin story. Nonetheless, I count on his love. I have faith in my children. I hope and pray that they will grow up holy and happy and will always love me as they do now, but I cannot see into the future.

I struggle to put certainty aside and to live an uncomfortably uncertain faith. I'm in conflict with myself. The sounds of internal battle have almost always echoed in my interior castle, but these, I have to hope, have mostly been signs of a healthy living faith, and not the noises of its injury and death. In my soul, hope has fought with suspicion, questions have parried final answers, and doubt and assent have appeared to play the game of thrones.

Such conflicts accompany me on the road, still. There's a wandering vagrant in every steadfast pilgrim, or so it seems to me. Faith involves walking in darkness; believing without seeing; and taking each step in fear, trembling, and hope. The point of faith is not to overcome or resolve these difficulties, but to live them out in love and in hope, in relationships with others and with God. Resolving them, one way or another, spells the death of faith. Both absolute certainty and absolute skepticism extinguish its fire.

22

Shattered Worlds

A year after we lost Vivian, we heard news that close friends of my wife's family had unexpectedly lost their thirty-six-week-old daughter after an emergency C-section. The baby had no heartbeat at her birth, and while the medical professionals were able to restart her heart, she passed away shortly after being flown to a big-city hospital. Neither parent was able to be with her when she passed.

I cannot say whether it is worse to lose a child knowing ahead of time that time is terribly limited, as my wife and I did, or to lose a child all of a sudden, with no warning and no expectation, as this couple experienced. I have no interest in knowing. I took the news harder than I would have expected, feeling grief and anger, especially anger, which I did not feel at my own loss. I felt sick for them, for the insurmountable devastation that tore at their hearts and will always pain their steps in life.

Though I could never forget the treasured moments of our fifteen hours with Vivian, nor her last gasps for air that passed between her parched, tender lips, I strangely felt as though I had yet to experience her life and death, as if all that we went through had yet to occur. I felt altogether unprepared for what took place in the past. I still do, and I can't escape or explain this feeling. It comes upon me strongest when I hear word of unexpected loss.

I seem to be, simultaneously, present now and lost in time years ago. At times my memories, the passage of time, and the world around me all seem unreal, like a half-worked, unwritten story muddily imagined in the mind of an author. I experience fear that I won't have the strength to endure the heartache and loss or the heart to enjoy the outpouring of love for which my soul yearns.

Often I remember some moment from Vivian's incredibly short life, and when I dwell upon those memories, her life flashes before my eyes. It's strange: our time together was so brief I could not come to know her personality—her character, her interests, her likes and dislikes—and yet despite all this, and while she was missing the top of her skull, she was to me then and remains to me now a whole person: Complete, a world made, a life lived, a story told. Not as complete as it should have been. Not as long a life as I would call fair or just or right. But there it was, and here I remember it and struggle to tell it.

It has been important for me to tell Vivian's story, short as it was. I feel as though I have been able to give her life additional meaning. By sharing her world, I have hoped that her life has touched the lives of others and that, paradoxically, her life has been touched in return. Telling her story has also been a way that I have sought to find wholeness in my shattered world.

23

Communities of Faith

The rain had departed in time for the young man and his best friend to take a walk he had carefully planned. They set out in the afternoon, dressed warmly to ward off the chilly October wind, and passed through the neighborhood, with few words and long silences between them. An overcast sky gave a bleaker hue to old houses colored in faded and peeling paint. Only the leaves, nearing the end of their lives, had the richness of living color. If the setting could have seen into the man's heart, it would have exploded in radiance—sidewalks erupting in silvers and grays, the sky overhead shining blue and golden, the faded houses vibrant and alive with reds and greens and whites, as if wood and brick and stone were the merry, moving lights of Christmas.

They neared the end of the road, but a path down the hill toward downtown began before them. This they took, under trees, next to mud, and down narrow steps that turned round and about until the ground leveled once again. The man checked his pocket repeatedly to make sure the item he secretly held had not fallen out or taken flight. His jaw trembled both from the cold air and from his nerves.

After a few blocks, they arrived at an old French Renaissance church of sandstone brick, bell towers, and reddish-brown domes. They found warmth inside, sitting in a wooden pew next to a large pillar, their eyes passing over the communion rail, Italian statues, and marble altars, then attentive to the mysteries of the rosary depicted in grand stained-glass windows. They knelt and prayed and breathed solemnly, preparing for Mass.

The church was still empty but for them. They had time for solitude, and in those quiet moments on their knees, the man took the ring from his pocket, presented it to his beloved, and proposed. She answered with whispered joy. Overheated by their overflowing hearts, they walked hand in hand outside to cool themselves in cold wind.

Eight months later, I married Genece in this same church. We began our life together as husband and wife within a community of faith and within a sacred space that we all shared. Members of religious communities were also present: priests, Franciscan sisters in habits, and a brother robed in black who would correct my slow dancing at the reception. Shortly after our marriage celebration, we packed our belongings and drove from the Ohio River valley to the northern outskirts of San Antonio, Texas, where I had moved a year before. At the time, I taught at a parish college-preparatory school and so was already a member of a parish, but as a newly married man, I rejoined the community, this time not as an individual, but as a member of a family, a little community ourselves.

In our time together, my wife and I have worshiped within very different parish communities: a university chapel known for its charismatic spirituality; a much more traditionalist Anglican Use church marked by Shakespearean prayers, altar rail, and rood screen; and a rapidly growing parish, numbering members in the tens of thousands who gather for Mass in a temporary facility with movable chairs and no kneelers. Each place has mediated our relationship with God in a unique way. Each community has had its own special traditions of imagining God, interpreting his word, and living the Catholic faith.

When my wife and I said our vows, we did not know and could not know where our life together would lead. We had to trust each other to stay true to our vows and to each other. That trust—that act of faith—has to continue, and for us it has. We remain one, the same, yet creatively new, a growing unity forged and strengthened by faith. To an extent, all communities are like this: they all, at least implicitly, come together and stay together in creative fidelity to their purpose and to those who share it. Faith leads one into communion with others and persists as the force binding the community together as one.

Communities are often based on some stated agreement—a statement of vows, a profession of faith, a signed lease, or recited prayers, for example—but this does not unify a community in actual practice. Spouses say vows, but then some cheat. Residents of an apartment agree in writing to respect the space of others and then blast their music so loudly that you can hear the lyrics perfectly even when you're in the shower. (Yeah, this happened.) Your registering at some parish office offers no guarantee that you will always remain with it, keep it in your heart, or seek its fulfillment (or it, yours).

For a community to love, its members must have faith in the community and be faithful to it. If you are truly part of a community, then your departure will be felt. What you brought to the community will be lost and not regained, for only you could bring it. Your influence may persist, but your presence will fade, and the community will become something other than what it was. Were everyone to depart, the community would vanish into memory.

Some communities are communities *of faith*: they exist to nourish and nurture the life of faith that underlies all true relationships. This ought to be a purpose of religious communities, but it can also be a purpose found within families and neighborhoods and playgroups and other communal organizations. It is a task my wife and I set for our own family, and while our private family life is distinct from the church, we understand our marriage and family as a state of life within the church. We strive to grow together in the virtues of faith, hope, and love.

Given the frantic nature of life, Genece and I are not as effective at our children's religious education as we'd like to be. We don't reinforce our son's weekly faith formation lessons as often as we should. He brings home a folder with worksheets and projects, and they get forgotten until we're emptying the folder the morning of his next Sunday-school class. We're more effective, I think, at instilling in our children a Christian imagination. We don't relegate our family's relationship with God to the Sabbath. We answer our son's questions and encourage him to ask them.

Once, in the midst of playing with some action figures at the dining room table, Jonathan asked us why God made human beings. In response, I told him that God wanted other beings who were capable of love to share in his love.

"Basically, it's all about love," I said.

"Oh," he answered, unimpressed, and continued to have one action figure pummel the other. "Why can't it all be about battles?"

That's one way of interpreting the universe, I thought. A while later, though, we overheard him playing with action figures, this time having the good guy give the bad guy a chance to atone and join the good side.

By being part of a church, we transcend our own family life and participate in a universal family. On its own, the notion of one human family makes little sense to me. Faith cannot be given or received from everyone. I cannot have faith in strangers I will never meet and whose decisions will probably have no bearing on my life. They have no way of hearing or accepting promises from me. I know of them only abstractly. I may as well trust the promises of rocks and streams I see when out for a stroll or a bicycle ride. However, if love is more than an act of individual wills, if it is a being itself in which we participate by being in love, then faith in this being of love may perhaps unite us with all those who share it and live in it.

With hope, I pray that all people will love and that by loving they will become one with one another and with me. I pray that this shared being-in-love unites the dead, the living, and the not yet born into an eternal community, a mystical body of the being of love itself. I further pray that this mystical community may subsist in all communities. I must hope for these intentions because they elude my sight and my understanding. They are uncertain—dreams glanced at through the dim, fragmented glass of shattered experiences and the stories we tell to make sense of them.

24

Worlds in Communion

I once came inches from a gruesome death. My mom and my stepdad were returning from a retreat. Seeing them arriving and excited to greet them, I ran over to the double-wide driveway gate that blocked their entering, grabbed hold of the metal bars, and began moving it along the railings that kept it attached to the wall. The gate was a six-foot-high chain-link fence with bars for support and wooden slats for privacy. It was very heavy, especially for me, a child small and scrawny for his age. As the gate neared the end of the railing, it unexpectedly detached. Joy at seeing their happy son turned to panic when this very large gate fell over and right on top of me. I could have been crushed. My parents thought I had been and screamed my name.

I was perfectly fine, lying comfortably under it and between bars, but my parents couldn't see this. They were unbearably frightened until they got the gate off of me and confirmed that I hadn't been paralyzed, squashed, or otherwise harmed. In the meantime, their panic didn't make perfect sense to me. *I'm fine*, I thought. *What's with all the fuss?*

For my parents, this was a moment of heart-stabbing fear that they'll never forget. It is seared into their souls. If one of them were to tell you the story I just related, it would differ substantially from my telling because it would be told from the perspective and emotions of a parent seeing a beloved child possibly killed. Perspective matters for the truth we see.

So do our dispositions. When my son was two years old and enthusiastic about the fun of walking, I had him outside in the yard. He strutted up to a large red ant hill, looked down at it, noticed it for what it was, ignored my warning, and stepped right on it—while wearing sandals. He wailed as ants swarmed his foot and bare leg. I quickly grabbed him and picked him out of the pile, removed the sandals, and brushed the biting ants from his skin. Many of them landed on my leg and began biting me. My wife heard the wails and came out the back door screaming for her son: "What's happened? What's wrong?" She saw the boy crying and in pain, and her heart went out to him. I, on the other hand, was admonishing him then and there: "This is what happens when you step on ant hills, son!" I had little sympathy for him because I knew he was feeling the consequences of something he did stupidly and deliberately. My wife and I were looking at the same scene, but we saw it differently and interpreted it differently: she as a moment for pity, I as a moment for scolding. As the boy was unable to walk for the next two days, I suppose my wife had the better sight and understanding.

In telling these stories, I have not told you what happened *as it actually happened*. Not that I've lied, mind you. I've put the experiences into words and words into sentences on the basis of how I remember and interpret the events. To tell a story is to build a world.

The biblical authors each uniquely perceived and interpreted the world in which he lived. They had specific purposes and audiences in mind when composing what we now know as the Bible. Each author created a distinct world presented to his audience, and these separate worlds were later brought together, each reinterpreted and understood in a new way, as worlds within a larger universe. This universe presented by the whole of sacred Scripture is one we as readers can enter not entirely unlike the way we enter into the fantasy worlds of Middle-earth or Hogwarts or Ivalice.

I would describe the Bible not as one world, but as a community of worlds. As truth is revealed and disclosed through these textual worlds, I would argue that we should think of truth as both one and many.

We can speak of truth as one thing, as it is in itself apart from all thought about it. We can refer to truth in this way, but in practice, no such truth enters our experience. We perceive reality from where we stand and interpret reality by way of our dispositions, presuppositions, and ideas about it. We then take these limited perceptions and interpretations and formulate them into words based in part on our purpose and our audience.

From the works of these words emerge worlds of meaning. These in turn are approached and interpreted relative to some situation or other—the worlds of the audience. These perceptions and interpretations and works and worlds may all be true, but the truth of them, taken together, cannot be combined into one coherent final super truth, not without abstracting their meaning and mentally destroying the worlds that gave this meaning birth.

J. R. R. Tolkien and J. K. Rowling created worlds of fantasy. Both of their worlds are arguably true, not in a literal sense, but in the sense that they each reveal something true of the human condition. Both even speak to some of the same truths. Nonetheless, these two worlds cannot be reduced to mere statements about the truths they convey, as if the stories were mere aesthetic coating over core philosophical lessons, and they cannot be married into one grand story. The individual stories would lose their coherence and soundness of meaning if Aragorn were to show up in Snape's classroom or Dobby the house-elf were to attend the Council of Elrond. The universe of fiction is a plurality of worlds, each of which, if true, is true in its own way.

What applies here also applies to the fields of history and science, philosophy and theology. It would be nonsensical to meld Augustine's *Confessions* with Aquinas's *Summa* even if both are theologically true. Each is a separate and distinct project, true in itself but also relative to the situations in which it came to be. These works may speak to the eternal and the absolute, but they do so relatively and subjectively.

By faith I affirm objective and absolute truth, but I deny that any way of perceiving, understanding, or formulating truth is purely objective or absolute. As Merold Westphal notes, we are not God, and we do not see reality as God sees it.[10] We speak about truth relative to who we are, what we are, where we are, when we are, and how we are; so there is always a relative and subjective aspect to our pursuit and attainment of truth. If we speak of our works as being truth, then there really are many truths because there are many works.

The worldview I'm describing is sometimes called pluralism. Truth does not exist in some kind of pure, essential realm untouched by history—not for us anyway. If such a place does exist (the mind of God?), not even the wisest of us has unmediated access to it. There is no encounter with truth that does not pass through perception and interpretation. Because no one can see the whole, no one can reach a final understanding of any part. For us, there is no truth untouched by the productivity of thought—by the building of worlds. As there are many standpoints for perception and situations informing interpretation, there can be no one be-all and end-all way of thinking the truth or thinking about truth. Rather, truth emerges in the meeting and transformation of worlds.

For all my church's dogmas, doctrines, and definitive teachings, it provides no singular interpretation of either Scripture or tradition. There is no such thing to be had. My church is home to diverse communities that approach the deposit of faith in their own special way, emphasizing various aspects of the life of faith and dwelling on different truths with various focuses. Every Catholic parish I have attended, from California to Delaware, Wisconsin to Texas, embodies the same Catholic faith in a manner unlike every other.

Truth remains always ahead of the individuals and the communities that pursue it and practice it, so we have to keep on the move, our eyes open to the unexpected and our hearts welcoming other individuals and communities on the road, residing in towns and palaces, and roaming in the wilderness. This pursuit is risky business. You never know whose world will shatter your own and leave you grabbing the scattered pieces to make something new. As Bilbo Baggins learned by venturing beyond the Shire, when you step into another world, the world you return to will not be the same one you left. Even if everything remains as it was, you will have changed, and so everything will not be the same for you.

And that is the point: personal transformation, conversion, and growth. Throughout this book I have spoken of the fragmentation of my life and of the human condition, framing these fragments as shattered parts of a former whole. What if we reconsider them as worlds we can enter and share with others? I think this is what happens when we strive to see the whole through the fragments before us.

My mother and father each came from different religious worlds. When they separated, their homes each became a separate world for me. I cannot reconcile my parents' accounts of their divorce anymore than I can combine my mom's Catholicism with my dad's Buddhism. Worlds may collide, they may affect one another as the moon affects the tide, but they are not Lego sets, easy to break apart and build into a superstructure in which every piece fits and has a place.

The brokenness of my life cannot be repaired, not fully. Healing cannot always come from putting back together what once was whole. I cannot remarry my parents or give them a shared religious faith. I cannot give Francis Estel a beating heart. I cannot return my father from the grave or call him now on the phone. I cannot look to God to do any of these tasks. They are not to be done. Some I would not want to be done. Because my mom and dad divorced, I now have a new family with wonderful siblings and a wonderful stepdad.

The best I can do now is not allow all of my life's fragments to remain fragments. I have to see them anew as meaningful wholes, as doors to distinct worlds, places where I may seek to learn and love and be loved. I have to bring them together and allow myself to be transformed by them and made more whole.

I live and journey in many worlds: my own home with my wife and children; the lives of my friends and families; the eternal community of my church. I enter a world of meaning every time I take a book off the shelf, watch a movie, or play a story-driven video game. When I browse the Internet, I am touched by people and places and ideas far from my own location. All these worlds change my own, I hope for the good.

Sometimes, however, events threaten to destroy the worlds we've built to make sense of our lives. Some disasters shake our faith, split it to its core, and leave us uncertain about where to turn. Where do we go from there?

Epilogue

I am a man broken, beyond repair but not beyond hope. I am a son who has failed his parents but desires to do better. I am a husband who struggles with the faith to love but in so doing has found happiness. I am a father of the living and the dead, praying for the strength to endure loss and loneliness and the unseen future. My faith, such as it is, keeps me moving and looking ahead.

In the fall of 2005, I came home from work exhausted and ready for a quiet evening. Genece said she had something to show me. I said sure and then went into the bedroom to change out of my work clothes because I had been at the school all day surrounded by germy children. She brought me a pregnancy test. It was positive.

"Well, that's interesting," I said with a nervous chuckle. "I'm . . . I'm not sure I'm ready for this." We had lost the first pregnancy not long before this revelation, and I was apprehensive.

Apprehensive, but hopeful.

My faith was soon tested. Genece began bleeding heavily in the seventh week, and we were all but absolutely certain that we were losing this child as well. I didn't see how in the little world of the womb the embryo could survive. We scheduled a sonogram, this time expecting to see no sign of a heartbeat, our hopes already diminished. We just needed verification in case a D&C would be once again required to remove the deceased.

Instead of stillness, we saw a strong heartbeat. Somehow the little jellybean had survived conditions in the womb I was certain should have killed him.

The bleeding continued, and Genece had to be on strict bed rest. Every morning, I brought a cooler to her bedside with breakfast and lunch. At six in the morning and six in the evening, I administered shots of progesterone. If your beloved still loves you after you've stuck her with needles for weeks on end, you know you've got a keeper.

Genece's sacrifices bore fruit: our firstborn, a son, strong and fat, whom we named Jonathan.

Jonathan's life exemplifies for me the strength of faith and the impotence of certainty. His fate could have been different, of course, and that's why I needed faith.

I cannot be certain of what joys and sorrows the future will bring or what really transpired in my past. I struggle right now with doubts about God, my religious community, and the real meaning of my life and my loves.

When these doubts threaten to overpower me, I recall standing next to Genece, the two of us together looking joyfully at the healthy beating heart of our son.

Endnotes

1. See Richard Kearney, *On Stories* (London: Routledge, 2002), 4.

2. Ilia Delio, *The Humility of God: A Franciscan Perspective* (Cincinnati: St. Anthony Messenger Press, 2005), 57.

3. St. Francis of Assisi, *Francis and Clare: The Complete Works*, trans. Regis J. Armstrong and Ignatius C. Brady (New York: Paulist Press, 1982), 63.

4. John D. Caputo, *On Religion* (New York: Routledge, 2001), 1.

5. Delio, *Humility of God*, 25.

6. Paul Ricoeur, *History and Truth*, trans. Charles A. Kelbley (Evanston, IL: Northwestern University Press, 1965), 56.

7. Gabriel Marcel, *Creative Fidelity*, trans. Robert Rosthal (New York: Fordham University Press, 2002), 68.

8. If you're looking for a philosophical overview of alterity, you can't do better than Brian Treanor's *Aspects of Alterity: Levinas, Marcel, and the Contemporary Debate* (New York: Fordham University Press, 2006).

9. See *The Cloud of Unknowing and Other Works*, trans. Clifton Wolters (London: Penguin Books, 1978).

10. See Merold Westphal, *Whose Community? Which Interpretation?* (Grand Rapids, MI: Baker, 2009).

Acknowledgments

My thanks to Jonathan and Mirielle for your patience while I attended to writing this book. To Genece for your love, support, and feedback, and for sharing this story with me. To my parents for helping me remember my story. My deepest gratitude to Paul Campbell, SJ, Joe Durepos, Steve Connor, Vinita Wright, Andrew Yankech, and everyone at Loyola Press for believing in this project. A big thank you to Vicky Cardoney, Rev. Timothy Heines, David Utsler, E. D. Kain, and to my blogging friends at The League of Ordinary Gentlemen and at Vox Nova. Your inspiration and criticism does not go unnoticed.

About the Author

Kyle R. Cupp has a BA in English and MA in philosophy from Franciscan University of Steubenville, Ohio. He is an independent writing and editing professional with extensive experience working in a Catholic environment as a teacher, administrator, and director of outreach ministries. He is married and a father of three.

Continue the Conversation

If you enjoyed this book, then connect with Loyola Press to continue the conversation, engage with other readers, and find out about new and upcoming books from your favorite spiritual writers.

Visit us at **LoyolaPress.com** to create an account and register for our newsletters.

Or scan the code on the left with your smartphone.

Connect with us through:

 Facebook
facebook.com
/loyolapress

 Twitter
twitter.com
/loyolapress

 YouTube
youtube.com
/loyolapress